Eyes to See, Ears to Hear

Eyes to See, Ears to Hear

An Introduction to
Ignatian Spirituality

David Lonsdale, S.J.

A Campion Book

Loyola University Press
Chicago

244.07
LO E

Loyola University Press
3441 North Ashland Avenue
Chicago, Illinois 60657

First published in 1990 by Darton Longman and Todd, Ltd.
89 Lillie Road, London SW6 1UD

Cover engraving: Mary Evans Picture Library

Library of Congress Cataloging-in-Publication Data

Lonsdale, David.
 Eyes to see, ears to hear: an introduction to Ignatian spirituality/
David Lonsdale.
   p. cm.
 Reprint. Originally published: London: Darton, Longman &
Todd, 1990.
 Includes bibliographical references and index.
 ISBN 0-8294-0721-9
 1. Ignatius, of Loyola, Saint, 1491–1556. 2. Spirituality—
History—16th century. I. Title.
BX4700 L7L64 1991
248.3—dc20   91-13247
               CIP

For my parents
Eileen and Edward Lonsdale
with love and gratitude

CONTENTS

ACKNOWLEDGEMENTS

After seven years as a student at a Jesuit school and more than twenty-five years as a member of the Society of Jesus I am clearly heavily in debt to a cloud of witnesses who have taught me about Ignatian spirituality. They are far too numerous to mention by name but I would like to express my thanks here to all who have contributed to this book: my fellow Jesuits and those teachers, retreat directors, homilists, spiritual guides and friends who as followers and companions of Jesus have shown me what it means to go along with Ignatius. I would also like to thank my colleagues at the Institute of Spirituality, Heythrop College, who allowed me time to write when other work was pressing and encouraged me when my enthusiasm flagged. I am grateful to Tom Shufflebotham SJ, Gerry W. Hughes SJ and Michael Ivens SJ for reading the book in manuscript and offering helpful suggestions for its improvement.

David Lonsdale SJ

INTRODUCTION

Ignatian spirituality has become widely popular recently among lay Christians, members of religious congregations and clergy in Europe and North America. This has come about largely through a broader dissemination of the practice of individually-guided retreats and various forms of 'retreats in daily life'. More and more people too are taking time to make the full Ignatian Spiritual Exercises, seeking spiritual direction for themselves or taking it up as a ministry. Others are becoming involved in working in a committed way for the kingdom of God as a result of an Ignatian stimulus or inspiration. These developments also cross traditional denominational boundaries: the groups of people involved include Roman Catholics, Anglicans, Methodists, Lutherans, Presbyterians, United Reformed Church members and Quakers.

I decided to write this book because, as I looked round for material with which to help people to find their way into Ignatian spirituality, I could not find an introductory work that I could put into their hands to guide their first steps and sketch out for them, without going into great detail, an overall picture. This book claims to do no more than that: to offer for thoughtful and interested Christians without any specialized knowledge an introduction to the way of living Christian discipleship that is associated with the name of Ignatius Loyola. If others who know and love Ignatian spirituality also read it and find something of value in it for themselves, that will be a bonus for me and I shall, of course, be glad to have made that contribution.

As an introduction, however, this is not a historical study, a look at Ignatius and his spirituality in the setting of the sixteenth century. That is an important task but not one for which I am well

1

qualified. What I am trying to do is to describe and discuss the ways of being a disciple of Jesus that have come down to us from Ignatius Loyola and are with us today. I am attempting to interpret Ignatius's spirituality in terms of some of the questions, needs, searchings and demands of our own times.

I should say that by spirituality I mean a way of living. We often take for granted that spirituality has to do entirely with such activities as prayer, worship, charitable or other 'good' works, the sacraments, making retreats and so on. Those activities are obviously an important part of any 'spirituality', but they are not the whole picture. In this book I am assuming that by spirituality we mean living in a certain way, and that this includes all the activities that make up the complex reality we call life. Christian spirituality, as I understand it, means primarily the attempt to give an orientation to the whole of one's daily living under the influence of the Spirit of Christ and the gospel.

That is one meaning of spirituality and it obviously includes the full range of events and activities, such as conversion, prayer, worship, that we usually associate with the meaning of the word. But it can also include other aspects of life such as falling in love, having children, bringing up a family, looking for a job, earning a living, playing games, relaxing and so on. For Ignatius the flurry of daily life is where we grow towards God. Activities like prayer, worship or contemplation clearly have an important place in this wider sense of spirituality as a way of living, but theirs is not necessarily the most important place. As we move towards God we search for ways of integrating the various elements that make a 'spirituality' into a harmonious whole. What is important is that all these elements of daily life take their tone, colouring and direction from the abiding presence of the Spirit of God who lives in and among us for the sake of the kingdom.

There is another meaning to the word spirituality however, which we should take note of. Our attempts to give a particular orientation to the whole of life under the influence of the gospel usually imply that we also have at least an underlying implicit understanding of what we take to be the purpose and meaning of human life in the setting of the created world. In Christian spirituality this understanding of the world in relation to God is supplied, through faith and experience, by reflection on the story of God's dealings with God's people. And this provides us with our second, more theoretical meaning of spirituality, which has to do with how we understand life rather than with how we actually live. In an integrated life, of course, the two are hardly separable: our understanding underpins the way we live and our actions and lifestyle are expressions of what we understand life and the world to be in relation to God.

The term 'Ignatian spirituality' as I have used it in this book includes both of these meanings. Ignatius lived his life in a certain way in interaction with the world around him and in relation to God. And we have received from him a way of living out our own Christian discipleship in our own circumstances which are in many respects markedly different from his. That is 'spirituality' as a way of living. But Ignatius's lifestyle was also increasingly guided by a particular way of understanding human life in relation to God, and Ignatius himself in his writings put this understanding into words. That is 'spirituality' as a vision of life based on faith, and we have to interpret this too for our own circumstances and times, and express it in our own terms. I have tried to introduce the non-specialist reader to Ignatian spirituality both as a way of living and as embodying a particular understanding of human life in relation to God.

Ignatian spirituality or Jesuit spirituality?

Ignatius Loyola was the founder of the Society of Jesus, a religious order in the Roman Catholic Church which at present numbers about 25,000 men. And it is all too easy to assume that when we talk about Ignatian spirituality we mean nothing more than the way of life of this religious order – 'Jesuit spirituality'. The two are in fact not quite the same. The Society of Jesus and its way of life are one particular embodiment of Ignatian spirituality, but they are not the only form in which Ignatian spirituality exists. Ignatian spirituality is prior to Jesuit spirituality and in a sense more fundamental. A single melody or line of music can appear in a variety of different forms: by itself, as the line of a song, orchestrated, arranged and rearranged, as the basis of a set of variations and so on, in many different shapes and settings. Ignatian spirituality is the original melody; Jesuit spirituality is one particular form or arrangement in which it has appeared. Ignatian spirituality has ways of acting, principles, attitudes, a foundation for living which are to some extent embodied in the life of the Society of Jesus but are not confined to that. You do not have to be a Jesuit to live Ignatian spirituality. On the contrary I hope to show clearly that what Ignatius has to offer as a way of being a disciple of Jesus is applicable to many forms of Christian life, whether lay, religious or ordained.

A note on sources

I have made use of some of the extant documents that date from Ignatius and his associates. These are obviously very valuable as they give us many insights into Ignatius in the context of his own time. But it is also important to recognize their limitations, and, as with any historical documents, to see that we inevitably read them from our own standpoint. Of the writings that we have, the following are the best known in English translation.

The Autobiography[1]

This is Ignatius's account of his own life up to the time of the founding of the Society of Jesus soon after he and his companions had arrived in Rome in 1538. After repeated requests from his community in Rome, Ignatius dictated this story in stages to Luis Gonçalves da Câmara not long before he died in 1556. A certain amount of mystery surrounds this document and the circumstances in which it was written. Da Camara was an enthusiastic admirer of Ignatius and well-suited to this task in that, according to his contemporaries, he had extraordinary powers of memory. But we do not know, for example, what led Ignatius finally to agree to dictate his story after so many hesitations and procrastinations. Nor do we know what exactly remains of Ignatius's own words and how much of the text is the writer's summary or reconstruction of what Ignatius said. Moreover the Autobiography is only partial in that it has hardly anything to say about the last sixteen years of Ignatius's life, the crucial formative years for the Society of Jesus. All of these factors affect our interpretation of the Autobiography and the weight that we give to it.[2]

The Letters

Ignatius was a prodigious letter-writer and about 7000 of his letters are still extant. There are two main selections in English,[3] and there is some overlapping between them. Hugo Rahner's collection contains very full accounts of the circumstances in which the letters were written and the people to whom they were addressed. When we are reading the letters of Ignatius we have to remember that from 1547 onwards he employed a succession of secretaries culminating in Juan Polanco, and it is not always possible to know whether we are reading Ignatius's own words or a letter written by the secretary from a rough draft, notes or instructions given to him by Ignatius himself.

The Spiritual Exercises[4]

Ignatius worked on the text of the *Spiritual Exercises* over a period of many years, correcting and reworking different sections, and we have a manuscript of a Spanish version of the *Exercises* with corrections in his own hand. Ignatius arranged for a Latin translation of the *Spiritual Exercises* to be published.

The Constitutions of the Society of Jesus[5]

Ignatius was still working on this document, in consultation with other Jesuits, up to the time of his death in 1556, and a definitive version was published later. One of the important factors that we have to take into account when we read the *Constitutions* is that in the space of sixteen years the number of members of the Society rose astonishingly from a handful to one thousand. This must have imposed on Ignatius a task of constant rewriting and revision, since recommendations and structures appropriate for a small band of men, most of whom know each other personally, are not necessarily suited to a cast of thousands scattered through the world.

The Spiritual Diary[6]

At certain periods of his life Ignatius kept a diary in which he wrote down each day what he experienced in his prayer. This helped him in making important decisions. Two fragments of this diary have survived, covering the period 2 February 1544 to 27 February 1545. This was a time when Ignatius was writing the Constitutions of the Society of Jesus, and he used his diary as part of the process of making some crucial choices about its way of life.

A Note on Terminology

I am using italics for the book title or the text itself (e.g. *Spiritual Exercises* or *Exercises*); roman to refer to the process of giving or making the Exercises in full (e.g. Spiritual Exercises or Exercises); and lower case to refer to individual exercises or parts of the process (e.g. the exercises of the First Week).

There are other documents written by associates of Ignatius which tell the story of his life or give us a 'reading' of him. Historians and biographers have naturally made far more direct use of these than I have in this book, and have given us a picture of Ignatius that has become 'classic'. Very often however they have not asked of the sources the kind of critical questions that modern historical scholarship is now posing. The time has come for a biography of Ignatius that is more critically aware of these questions, of the particular slants and perspectives of the writers of those contemporary documents and of the circumstances surrounding their composition. This might be unlikely to alter the broad outlines of the portrait we have of Ignatius, but it would serve to highlight some so far neglected areas of his life, particularly the years 1540–1556. Until that biography is written, however, we have to be content for the purposes of this book with a 'classic' sketch of Ignatius the man. And that is the subject of the first chapter.

1 English translations of the Autobiography include: *St Ignatius' own Story*, tr. William J. Young SJ (Loyola University Press, Chicago, 1956/1980); *Inigo: original testament*, tr. William Yeomans SJ (Inigo Enterprises, London, 1985); *A pilgrim's journey: the Autobiography of Ignatius Loyola*, introd., tr. and comm. Joseph N. Tylenda SJ (Michael Glazier, Wilmington, Del. 1985).

2 Philip Endean SJ discusses the questions that these and other factors raise about accepted interpretations of Ignatius in 'Who do you say Ignatius is? Jesuit fundamentalism and beyond', *Studies in the spirituality of Jesuits*, vol. 19, no. 5 (November 1987).

3 *Letters of St Ignatius Loyola*, sel. and tr. William J. Young SJ (Loyola University Press, Chicago, 1959); *St Ignatius Loyola, letters to women*, ed. Hugo Rahner SJ (Nelson, London, 1960).

4 There are several translations of the *Spiritual Exercises* in English in current use: for example, Louis J. Puhl SJ (Loyola University Press, Chicago, 1950); A. Mottola (Doubleday, Image Books, 1964); and David L. Fleming SJ, *The Spiritual Exercises of St Ignatius: a literal translation and a contemporary reading* (Institute of Jesuit Sources, St Louis, 1978).

5 cf. *The Constitutions of the Society of Jesus*, tr. with introd. and comm. George E. Ganss, SJ (Institute of Jesuit Sources, St Louis, 1970). Cited as *Constitutions*.

6 The most recent English translation of this difficult text is: *Inigo: discernment log-book. The spiritual diary of Saint Ignatius Loyola*, ed. and tr. Joseph A. Munitiz SJ (Inigo Enterprises, London, 1987).

1

IMAGES OF IGNATIUS

If we are to appreciate the relevance of Ignatian spirituality to ourselves in our own age we need to have some understanding of Ignatius himself, the kind of man that he was in the setting of the times in which he lived. In this chapter I want to sketch an impression of Ignatius the man, but not by simply re-telling his story in a short form. The main events of Ignatius's life are well documented[1] and I am assuming that readers will have a basic knowledge of them. Here instead I am going to present Ignatius by way of a few major images: the would-be romantic hero, the courtier-soldier, the pilgrim and the evangelizer. These images were either important to Ignatius's explicit understanding of himself or else were significant influences in the formation of his mentality and outlook. And apart from the four I have mentioned there is another, less distinct but none the less significant image hovering in the background of Ignatius's life; a kind of shadow or anti-image. That is the figure of the career cleric, and to understand Ignatius more fully we must have a look at that figure too.

To some degree, of course, these images represent successive stages of Ignatius's life. He was a would-be romantic hero, a courtier and a soldier before he was a pilgrim; and the image of himself as an evangelizer apparently formed gradually through the pilgrim years and became fully effective only later, after his studies. But it would be a mistake to separate the images or stages rigidly one from another. It is not as though he entirely left behind the earlier images and their influence when he moved into a later phase. Features of what he once was remain permanent parts of his total personality and make a lasting contribution to the man of later years. As well as phases of a journey or process of growth, these different images are also like slides projected on to a screen. Each one separately has meaning and importance in its own right; but superimposed upon one another they form a more complex, interesting, composite picture to which each separate image makes its own special contribution. Or, to change the metaphor again, a painter will use several different layers of paint and varnish in the course of painting a portrait in order to produce the desired final picture. In the end some of these layers are no longer directly visible, and yet each one adds something distinctive to the picture and it would be a different portrait if any of them was left out. The images of would-be romantic hero, soldier, pilgrim and evangelist, along with the anti-image of the career cleric, do not add up to a detailed finished portrait of Ignatius but offer a not-inaccurate cartoon.

A would-be romantic hero

... without realising it he could spend two, three or even four hours on end thinking of it, fancying what he would have to do in the service of a certain lady, of the means he would take to reach the country where she was living, of the verses, the promises he would make her, the deeds of gallantry he would do in her service. He was so enamoured with all this that he did not see how impossible it would all be, because the lady was of no ordinary rank; neither countess, nor duchess, but of a nobility much higher than any of these. (Autobiography, 6)

As a young man Ignatius was greatly devoted to romances, the popular fiction of his day. A few years before he died, in the course of telling Luis Gonçalves da Câmara the story of his life, he said that on the road to Montserrat as he began his pilgrimage his head had been 'filled with the adventures of Amadis of Gaul and such books'. So he decided to make:

a watch of arms throughout the whole night, without ever sitting or lying down, but standing a while and then kneeling, before the altar of Our Lady of Montserrat, where he had made up his mind to leave his fine attire and to clothe himself with the armour of Christ. (Autobiography, 17)

As an eager young courtier, first in the household of Juan Velázquez de Cuéllar, Chief Treasurer of Castile, and later at the court of Don Antonio Manrique de Lara, Duke of Nájera and Viceroy of Navarre, Ignatius drank in and assimilated the mentality and many of the best and worst values embodied in his favourite reading. The literary world which this opened up to him is familiar enough: stories of groups of knights united in service of their king and companionship with one another; knights setting off alone or in a company in search of adventures; fantastic tales in which knights meet ogres, monsters, dragons and magicians as well as other knights in fierce and fatal fighting, often in order to rescue captured or spellbound ladies who are always, of course, young and beautiful; stories of magic and wonder, of passionate love, faithfulness and betrayal, in which knights perform amazing feats and undergo intense suffering for the sake of the lady whom they serve. Here Ignatius found a dream world in which he could become absorbed for hours on end, but also a system of values and models real enough to be guides for his own life and behaviour.[2]

Ignatius did not immediately abandon the outlook and ideals of the would-be knight-errant when he began to 'clothe himself with the armour of Christ'. At first his understanding of what this involved was inevitably crude. Readers of some of the less sophisticated of the romances would easily recognize and even applaud his tactics in his meeting with the Muslim soon after he left Loyola (Autobiography 14–16). Later Ignatius himself recognized this beginning of his pilgrimage as a time when he was 'still blind'; nevertheless he did have 'great desire to serve God to the best of his knowledge', and that was what led him on.

We should not assume that Ignatius appropriated only the superficial trappings of the romances and not their deeper ideals. Some at least of the more profound values which he held on to for a long time have some of their roots in the soil of the romances. At the beginning of the sixteenth century the feudal age was coming to an end even in the conservative regions of northern Spain. The romances, however, embody in an idealized form some of the best feudal values, and these ideals fired Ignatius's young imagination. One of the values that the romances idealized is the feudal relationship between a vassal-knight and the greater lord whom he served. Both the knight-vassal and the lord entered into this relationship voluntarily by way of a symbolic rite of homage. The basis of the relationship, in the best examples, was love. Both the knight and the king took on certain obligations towards each other on a basis of mutual friendship. For the knight this meant primarily deeds of service, giving help and advice when called upon, with the desire to distinguish himself in that service. The king, out of personal concern and interest, undertook to be the knight's leader and friend, offering maintenance and protection. In the ethical system that developed from this the most prized qualities for the vassal were fidelity, courage and a willingness to suffer in the lord's service, along with generosity towards the lord and the other knights. The lord was also admired for fidelity and generosity towards his vassal-knights.

This relationship and the qualities that it represented were among the ideals that Ignatius valued highly at the time of his conversion. They provided him with a model which he transferred to his following of Jesus. He became the vassal and knight-companion of Christ. He was not the first, of course, to use the model in that way. He came across it in his reading, because Vagad's preface to the *Flos Sanctorum*, which was one of only two books available to him to pass the time during his long and painful convalescence at Loyola, develops the theme of the saints as knights of God. But the *Spiritual Exercises* use romance and feudal language and images extensively, especially in the Call of the King and the Meditation on Two Standards. Though we do not find this language and these images much in Ignatius's writing outside the *Exercises*, they clearly represent values and qualities which were important to him around the time of his conversion, and his repeated revision of the *Exercises* never erased them.[3]

Though Ignatius later pronounced his absorption in dreams of chivalry as vain and worldly, some of the deeper values which these stories rather obscurely embody apparently influenced him more

11

than he imagined. Perhaps behind Ignatius's image of the Jesuit as a man who is able to travel to any part of the world in response to an urgent need and at the service of Christ there lurks the magical, colourful figure of the crusading knight-errant, ready to set out on adventures of mercy and help at the word of his king.

The courtier-soldier

'Whoever desires to serve as a soldier of God beneath the banner of the cross in our Society, which we desire to be designated by the name of Jesus, and to serve the Lord alone and the Church his spouse . . .'[4] As a young man Ignatius was both a courtier and a soldier, but we should remember that in sixteenth-century Spain these two careers were not clearly distinct. The shaping influences on Ignatius of the romances and of his ideals and experience as a courtier-soldier blend and work together. This is not surprising when we remember that they both arose within the cultural milieu of late-medieval feudal society, and that the romances often present more commonplace feudal relationships and values in a more intensified and idealized form.

Looking at the image of Ignatius the soldier however, we should keep in mind the differences between his age and ours, otherwise we will misunderstand the image. First, Ignatius was never embarrassed, as we now would be, at the use of military language to express his own, the Church's, the Society's or even Jesus's mission. Spain was different from other countries of Europe because 'the Moors', seen as infidels and traditional enemies of Christendom, were not people living in a faraway land but a powerful, hated presence in Spain itself for a long time before the Reconquest of 1492. And later in Ignatius's lifetime there were events which kept the crusading spirit alive. The great hero of the Reconquest, the 'Great Captain', was still chalking up victories in Italy, though not against 'the Moors', when Ignatius was in his teens. The Muslim pressure on Christendom continued by land and sea, and from time to time the greatest concern of the Emperor Charles and his brother King Ferdinand was to repel them. These campaigns were presented, albeit simplistically, as crusades. So there was a crusading spirit in the air while the king and his 'captains' tended to be cast in the role of the men who would lead the followers of Christ to victory over the infidels.[5]

When Spain, Portugal and other European countries colonized lands and peoples of Asia and Latin America by force, they unashamedly took Christianity with them and tried to compel the native peoples to accept it under threat of annihilation. Ignatius and his contemporaries did not share our modern sensitivity about colonialism and the linking of Christianity and conquest. The old crusaders turned into the new conquistadors. So when Ignatius depicts Jesus saying such things as 'It is my will to conquer all the world and all enemies' (Exx 96) he is just using the language of his time without having our modern sensitivities about its aptness. At least in his early days of serious discipleship, Ignatius saw any non-Christians as infidels who had to be conquered for Christ, and in this simply reflected current attitudes.[6]

Another important difference between Ignatius's age and ours lies in the meaning of the image of the soldier. We have to remember that in this Ignatius is closer to Agincourt than to Waterloo. In modern warfare we are used to thinking of enormous armies of hundreds of thousands of people being transported over great distances in mechanized forms of transport by land, sea or air. In Ignatius's time the armies were far smaller with far less complex structures and organization, and while the officers had horses the vast majority of the soldiers travelled on foot. The destructive power of the weapons used was far less, of course, and all men of Ignatius's rank had to be skilled in hand-to-hand combat. A soldier and especially an officer was less a small cog in a large machine than he would be in a modern army. The nature of the fighting and of his position of leadership was likely to demand from him a high level of initiative, skill in swordsmanship, the ability to inspire others by personal example, courage and bravery in the face of danger to his life and damage to his pride. Ignatius says of himself at Pamplona:

He was in a fortress which the French were attacking, and

although the others were of the opinion that they should surrender on terms of having their lives spared, as they clearly saw
there was no possibility of a defence, he gave so many reasons to
the governor that he persuaded him to carry on the defence
against the judgement of the officers, who found some strength
in his spirit and courage. (Autobiography, 1)

When Ignatius was injured, the others surrendered.

His life as a soldier offered Ignatius an experience of friendship
and close companionship. In wartime particularly, the lord and
his knights shared the same life: food, accommodation, often long
journeys together, and miseries as well as victories. They depended
upon one another for help, support and protection in real danger
of injury or death; they had to trust one another's loyalty and
collaborate closely in difficult and dangerous enterprises; all of this
depended upon and could create strong bonds of personal love and
friendship. It is clear from the *Exercises* that this kind of experience
coloured Ignatius's understanding of his relationship with Jesus
(Exx 96–100), and it probably also helped to give a foundation and
a shape to his association with his first companions. His characteristically laconic description of love in the Exercises evokes not so
much the knight's passionate devotion to his lady in the romances
as the perhaps more prosaic but none the less real commitment and
sharing of mind, heart and life between friends: 'love ought to
manifest itself in deeds rather than in words'; and:

> love consists in a mutual sharing of goods, for example, the lover
> gives and shares with the beloved what he possesses, or something
> of that which he has or is able to give; and vice versa, the beloved
> shares with the lover . . . Thus, one always gives to the other.
> (Exx 230)

Ignatius was a good friend and set a high value on friendship. He
described the group of himself and his companions as 'friends in
the Lord'. He kept many friends for many years, especially those
who had been good to him when he was a poor pilgrim, and kept
in touch with his friends, both women and men, by letter. Some of

his most beautiful letters are those written to friends, relatives of Jesuits or simply acquaintances, on occasions when he had received news of some event, whether joyful or sorrowful, that was important to them.[7] When Ignatius and his companions were trying to decide whether to bind themselves by obedience to one of their own number they took the deep friendship that had grown between them as a sign that they should try to preserve permanent bonds with each other.[8] In a letter from the East Francis Xavier tells how he carries his friends' signatures around with him next to his heart. Even a strongly worded letter of reproof from Ignatius to Diego Laínez, one of the early companions, could evoke in reply a moving testimony to the value Laínez set on Ignatius's friendship. When the behaviour of Simão Rodrigues, another early companion, became increasingly erratic and anarchic, Ignatius's affection and generosity towards him never failed. And when Ignatius came to write the *Constitutions* he saw friendship and keeping in contact by writing letters as the bonds which would unite the necessarily scattered members of the Society.[9]

Within the bonds of friendship Ignatius had the capacity and the freedom to give himself generously to serving other people, and he was delighted when he found that those around him were also magnanimous (cf. Exx 5). That is why he puts so much emphasis on having 'great desires' to serve God.[10] He saw himself as committed to Christ 'as one friend to another' (Exx 54; cf. Exx 224), and serving Christ eventually came to mean giving himself generously in the service of other men and women. Under his guidance his younger friends grew into, not servants of Ignatius but servants and friends of Jesus who, in companionship with one another, were ready to go to any part of the world in service of the Church and their fellow men and women. The soldier's desire to distinguish himself in service out of affection for his lord eventually turned into the desire to join and lead his companions in working for 'the (greater) praise and service of Christ our Lord', a phrase which is repeated in the Constitutions almost to the point of tedium.

Another quality which stood Ignatius in good stead as a soldier and which he took with him into his very different way of life was a kind of very imaginative daring. He had the ability, especially as regards the mission of the Society, to conceive, put into execution and carry through apparently impossible tasks; to respond in a courageous and often quite imaginative way to the needs of a situation. The far-sightedness, variety and daring of the missions of Jesuits set in motion within Ignatius's own lifetime in distant parts of the world are some indication of these qualities. They bear the mark of the man who advised fighting on against the odds at Pamplona and who dreamed of imitating the daring adventures of knights in the old romances.

The career cleric

As a younger son in a family of the lower nobility educated at the court of the Duke of Nájera Ignatius could have chosen to be a conventional career cleric. In fact there is some indication that for some time that is what he intended to become, or at least what his family intended for him. When as a young man he was accused at a trial he claimed clerical immunity, which indicates that he had already entered into a clerical state of some kind. His education at court provided him with both the background and the contacts to enable him to be appointed eventually to a bishopric, which might have led to pastoral or diplomatic and political roles at home or abroad in the expanding Spanish territories. The progression from courtier to soldier to bishop was by no means uncommon for younger sons who had a career to make for themselves.

Historians have frequently described the abuses brought upon the Church by the institution of career clerics: absentee bishops; neglect of catechesis and pastoral care in dioceses and parishes; bishops amassing personal fortunes at the expense of impoverishing local churches; ignorant and ill-trained clergy; a serious decline in preaching, teaching and the sacramental life.[11] Ignatius's conversion made him far more sensitive than before to these abuses and the scars they caused. And as he and his companions walked through Europe they met them over and over again at first hand in the many places through which they travelled.

It is not entirely surprising then that the image of the career cleric can be seen hovering in the background of the Spiritual Exercises. It is what Ignatius could have become but did not.[12] It represents perhaps a kind of 'shadow' in himself against which Ignatius reacted, as well as a primary cause of abuses in the Church. And career clerics among both secular clergy and religious were among the first people to whom Ignatius gave the Exercises. It is not unlikely then that this image lies behind, for example, the Meditation on Two Standards (Exx 136–48), the examples of the Three Classes of Men (Exx 149–57) and the Election generally:

> The first prelude is the narrative, which is of three pairs of men, and each of them has acquired ten thousand ducats, not solely or as they ought for God's love, and all want to save themselves and find peace in God our Lord, ridding themselves of the weight and hindrance to it which they have in the attachment for the thing acquired. (Exx 150)

Even before they formed the Society of Jesus, Ignatius and his companions were known as a band of 'reformed priests'. It was largely in response to the needs of the people in the Church that Ignatius formulated what he saw as the mission and style of life of the Society of Jesus. So the image of the career cleric also left its mark on Ignatius's selection of poverty as one of the important characteristics of Jesus and of good disciples of Jesus, even to the extent of asking those who make the Exercises to pray explicitly for poverty (Exx 146, 147). The same figures also seems to have influenced Ignatius in trying to make sure that Jesuits do not seek positions of power in the Church or in the Society,[13] and in his legislation on the kind of poverty appropriate to the Society as a body.[14]

The pilgrim

> Before reaching Montserrat he arrived at a large town where he bought the clothing he had made up his mind to wear when he went to Jerusalem. It was some sacking of a very loose weave

and a rough prickly surface, and he at once gave orders for a long garment reaching to his feet to be made of it. He bought a pilgrim's staff and a small gourd and attached it all to the mule's saddle. (Autobiography, 16)

In setting out as a pilgrim Ignatius was turning away definitively from the path of the career cleric and the soldier. His intention was to go to Jerusalem 'undertaking all the disciplines and abstinences which a generous soul on fire with the love of God is wont to desire' (Autobiography, 9). About what he would do with the rest of his life after that he was uncertain; he had a number of ideas, mostly inspired by his enthusiastic reading of the lives of the saints. One possibility was to spend the rest of his life as a penitent and ascetic in the Holy Land. As things turned out, on his way to Jerusalem he stayed for about ten months at Manresa and when he finally reached Jerusalem, seventeen months after leaving Loyola, he was allowed to stay there only twenty days.[15]

The image of himself as 'the pilgrim' was a very significant one for Ignatius. It was one of the images that he used to describe himself, and therefore gives us a key to how he understood himself. In his account of his own life, which he told to Luis Gonçalves da Câmara not long before he died, he constantly referred to himself as 'the pilgrim'. Something of the pilgrim's spirit and mentality seems to have stayed with him till the end of his life.

Ignatius's pilgrimage of course was more than just a physical journey inspired by a desire to see and touch the places where Jesus had lived. He was also a pilgrim of the spirit. This is how he later described himself at the time when he set out:

> He never took a spiritual view of anything, nor even knew the meaning of humility, or charity, or patience, or discretion as a rule and measure of these virtues. His whole purpose was to perform these great, external works, for so had acted the saints for God's glory, without thought of any more particular circumstance. (Autobiography, 14)

The man who arrived back in Spain from Jerusalem had changed much and the great significance that the pilgrim image had for Ignatius right through his life probably had to do with those changes. If we include the time at Manresa it was the most formative experience of his life, so that for our understanding of Ignatius, the pilgrim image is at least as significant as that of the would-be romantic hero or the courtier-soldier.

His pilgrimage was a time when Ignatius was surrendering to God the control of his own life. He was learning to allow himself to be led by God. And the story of his pilgrim years shows us a man struggling with a conflict between his propensity to anxiety and a growing trust in God. Little by little he learned to trust God profoundly, but it cost him much. Like the Hebrew prophets he loved symbolic actions, and his actions of leaving behind his sword and dagger, abandoning his mule to go on foot, and giving his fine clothes to a poor man (who was almost arrested on suspicion of having stolen them) meant that he was turning away from the things which till then had given him security and status, and trying to place all his trust in God's power and willingness to look after him. Though he was a courageous soldier and a romantic dreamer he was also a man subject to anxiety, especially as regards sin and God. So at Manresa there was a long period when he struggled with scruples and with a paralysing need to keep going over in his mind and re-confessing sins of the past, unable to trust that God had already forgiven him.[16] Several times during his pilgrimage, he suffered acute anxiety over money. His general practice at that time was to beg for money, and if he received more than he needed for his frugal essentials he would give the rest away to other needy people. When he was leaving Barcelona by sea he had an anxious debate with himself as to whether he should take with him some ship's biscuit as provision for the journey, or whether this would be a betrayal of his trust in the power and willingness of God to provide for him. Eventually he decided that it would be all right to take the biscuit with him. Then however another problem arose: he found five or six of the smallest Spanish coins of the time in his pockets, 'all that was left of what he had begged from door to door'. These he decided not to take with him, so he 'left them on a bench there on the seashore' (Autobiography, 36).

19

This incident illustrates his susceptibility to anxiety and scruples, and the fact that his pilgrimage, in which he sometimes seems to have had to force himself to trust the God whom he eagerly wanted to serve, was a school of trust for him. Though he probably never entirely lost his propensity to be anxious, as time went by his anxiety no longer paralysed him. As a result of his struggles during his pilgrimage he could later take up the most courageous projects for himself or on behalf of the Society with a more serene confidence in the power of God to bring to completion what God had already begun. If God had seen him safely through his pilgrimage, then God could be trusted.

Another feature of Ignatius's pilgrimage is the growth of extra-ordinary mystical gifts, some of which he describes in his Auto-biography (e.g. 28–31). The weeks of his stay at Manresa after his violent struggle with scruples were a time of special enlightenment. Characteristically his descriptions of what he experienced are not fulsome, but he was clearly convinced that the insights into such mysteries of faith as creation, the Trinity, the humanity of Christ and the Eucharist, which he had at that time, were extraordinary gifts:

> These things which he saw gave him at the time great strength and were always a striking confirmation of his faith, so much so that he has often thought to himself that if there were no scrip-tures to teach us these matters of faith, he was determined to die for them, merely because of what he had seen. (Autobiography, 29)

One incident in particular seemed to stand out in his memory as a 'peak' experience. It was while he was sitting quietly by the side of the river Cardoner, not far from Manresa, and:

> the eyes of his understanding began to be opened. It was not that he saw a vision but he came to understand and know many things, as well about spiritual things as about matters of faith and secular learning, and that with so strong an enlightenment that all things seemed quite new to him ... If he were to put

together all the helps God had given him and all the many things he had learnt in the whole of his sixty-two years, all these taken together would not, he thought, amount to what he had received on that single occasion. (Autobiography, 30)

Ignatius's experience appears to have had a mystical dimension to the end of his life. The gifts he received both deepened his sense of his own apostolic mission and that of the Society of Jesus, and encouraged and confirmed him in difficult decisions he had to face.

A pilgrim in the conditions in which Ignatius was a pilgrim needs two other qualities to an outstanding degree: first the ability to carry a project through to the end despite the most severe and unexpected obstacles, and secondly the ability to adapt to people and to circumstances. The torments that Ignatius was willing to suffer to have his leg straightened suggest that he already had the first quality before he set out for Jerusalem, and his journey gave him ample scope to exercise it. He was an extremely determined and persistent man.

As for the second quality, a pilgrim in those conditions is at the mercy in an extreme way of people and circumstances. He or she has to change and adapt constantly in response to events and people, and in the face of a thousand different obstacles learns how to choose the means which will lead to the envisaged goal. In a sense there are no unexpected circumstances because there are no expected ones. Choices have constantly to be made about situations that arise and, when necessary, new directions have to be taken, keeping always in mind the goal of the journey. These necessities contributed powerfully to Ignatius's education in spiritual discernment, which had already begun at Loyola (Autobiography, 7–8). Travelling slowly on a mule or on foot over long distances for months on end gives a person lengthy stretches of time for observation and reflection, whether of outer or inner worlds. No doubt Ignatius's ability to note and reflect on his own responses to people and events, which he had discovered at Loyola, was developed on the road. His constant desire during his pilgrimage was to 'find the will of God and have the courage to carry it out'.[17] His struggles with anxiety and scruples, the need to make choices about each stage on the journey and his surprising and disappointing discovery in Jerusalem that God apparently did not want him to spend a long time there, these and other circumstances were the ingredients of that search.

If the pilgrimage was an education in discernment it was also an education in freedom; the two go together. If the pilgrim is at the mercy of changing circumstances, it is also true that he or she has the freedom of the open road: to choose which direction to take, how quickly or slowly to move, when to travel and when to stay. Leaving Loyola, Ignatius already had a deep desire to spend his life serving God. But in trying to decide how he could best put this desire to effect he was guided at first by the examples of saints he had read about. Not that he had been a keen reader of saints' lives in his youth. But after he was wounded at Pamplona he returned to convalesce at Loyola and the only books he could lay his hands on there were *The life of Christ* by Ludolph of Saxony and 'a book of the lives of the saints, in Spanish' (Autobiography, 5). So he used to reflect, rather simplistically, in this way: 'St Dominic did this, therefore I must do it. St Francis did this, therefore I must do it' (Autobiography, 7). By contrast when he finally returned to Spain after having to leave Jerusalem, he could choose his next step on the basis of noting the pattern of what he believed to be God's leading in his own life rather than by others' example. This marks a decisive growth in the personal freedom necessary for spiritual discernment.

Later in his life Ignatius passed on to his companions elements of the pilgrim mentality and outlook. Some of them like Pierre Favre, Francis Xavier and Jeronimo Nadal spent years of their lives on the road, moving from place to place in response to requests and needs. And when Ignatius wrote the Constititions of the Society of Jesus he recommended that all Jesuit novices should also have the benefit of a pilgrim experience as part of their formation.[18] And the experience of being a pilgrim probably also accounts for the fact that when Ignatius is discussing ways and means of choosing missions and ministries that are appropriate to Jesuits he puts so much emphasis on discernment of spirits and the ability to respond flexibly to needs and circumstances, avoiding rigidity and crippling uniformity.[19] Time and again in the Constitutions too, Ignatius reinforces the need for constant reflection and discernment by laying down a guideline about what is to be done and then qualifying it by saying that this of course is alterable and choices are to take into account the differences of time and place. Contrary to popular belief flexibility and freedom, within a context of discernment, are hallmarks of Ignatius's legislation for his order.

The evangelizer: from Manresa to Rome

'After the pilgrim understood that it was not God's will that he remain in Jerusalem, he kept thinking on what he ought to be doing, and finally felt more inclined to study so as to be able to help souls' (Autobiography, 50). Ignatius's work of 'helping souls' falls into two distinct phases. The first takes in his pilgrimage and studies and ends with his election as head of the newly formed Society of Jesus in 1539; the second runs from that election to his death in 1556.

The principal change that came over Ignatius during his pilgrimage had to do with the direction his life should take. A distinct shift in emphasis took place which eventually brought very far-reaching effects. For most of his pilgrimage his main concern seems to have been with his own relationship with God and his own growth in this relationship rather than with placing himself at the service of others. It is true, of course, that during those pilgrim years he did spend time 'helping souls' when the chance arose, but his aim was mainly to go to Jerusalem in order to live a life of penance there. The pilgrim showed little concern at that time for the Church at large, little awareness of being a member of a worldwide community. After his enforced return from Jerusalem his new future gradually led him to two considerable changes in attitude. First he saw more clearly that his new aim should be to put himself at the service of other people in some way. And secondly, connected with that, he gradually began to attract and shape a band of companions who eventually grew to appreciate the value of living and serving others as a group rather than as solitary individuals. The pilgrim became an evangelizer and co-founder of a community at the service of the universal Church.

Back from Jerusalem then, he decided he would devote himself to 'helping souls', and for that he needed to study. So in his early thirties he went back to school to learn Latin, with the prospect of seven or eight years' study ahead of him.

Ignatius's life of evangelizing and 'helping souls' took different forms which varied according to the circumstances in which he found himself. As a pilgrim and at the beginning of his life as a student in Alcalá, Salamanca and Paris it was his practice to engage people in conversations with a view to catechesis and spiritual guidance. ' "We do not preach," replied the pilgrim, "but we speak familiarly of spiritual things with a few, as one does after dinner, with those who invite us." ' (Autobiography, 65). At the same time he started to give the Exercises to selected people, and eventually, after some false starts, a group of companions joined him and they tried to share a kind of common life.

At the end of his studies in Paris he returned home to Loyola for a visit and was immediately involved in evangelization and reform:

> As soon as he arrived, he made up his mind to teach the catechism daily to the children. But his brother made strenuous objection to this, declaring that nobody would come. The pilgrim answered that one would be enough. But after he began, many came faithfully to hear him, even his brother. (Autobiography, 88)

In addition he preached with success on Sundays and feast days, tried to rectify some gambling abuses and some matters that had to do with priests' concubines, made some better regular provision for the poor in the area and arranged for the Angelus to be rung three times a day so that the people could pray (Autobiography, 88–9).

As Ignatius and his companions walked from Paris through Italy to Rome, having put behind them once for all the possibility of going to Jerusalem, again their work among the people took different forms. When they stayed for some time in a city, as they did in Venice, Ignatius gave the Exercises, and they all worked in the hospitals, especially among the poorer people, looking after the sick and giving spiritual help where appropriate. When they were just passing through a town and not staying very long they preached in the streets, marketplaces and sometimes in the churches. In Vicenza four of them:

> went to four different piazzas on the same day and at the same hour, and began to preach, first by shouting out to the people and waving their hats at them. This style of preaching started a great deal of talk in the city; many were moved to devotion and supplied their physical needs with greater abundance. (Autobiography, 95)

Those were the days of Ignatius's direct involvement in evangelizing and 'helping souls'. The forms that this work took were not so much thought out beforehand as taken up in response to the needs of the places in which they found themselves, with a preference for work among the poor in hospitals and prisons and for teaching catechism to children. The variety of forms reflects the variety of needs in different places, and the range of different kinds of work that Ignatius himself successfully took up both in Rome and before he arrived there is a measure of the wide range of people with whom he was able to establish some kind of rapport.

The evangelizer: Rome

> After being ordained, he had decided to remain for a year without saying Mass, preparing himself and praying to Our Lady that she might be pleased to put him with her Son. One day then, a few miles outside Rome, in a church whilst he was praying, he felt such a change in his soul and saw so clearly that God the Father had put him with Christ his Son that he did not dare doubt about this fact that God the Father put him with his Son. (Autobiography, 96)

Ignatius and his companions were on their way to Rome when this

25

occurred, having been prevented by war from going to Jerusalem. They travelled in threes and Ignatius was with Pierre Favre and Diego Laínez. They were all uncertain about the shape their future would take.

Part of Ignatius's practice of discernment, which we will discuss more fully in Chapter 4, was to note 'peak' experiences and later, when he was faced with an important decision, to recall those peak experiences and allow them to shed light on the decision that was before him. This incident, which took place in the church of La Storta just outside Rome, is one of those peak experiences which Ignatius and his companions came back to repeatedly in their later discussions. There are several accounts of what happened: some of them say that Ignatius had a vision of Jesus carrying his cross, and understood that God wanted him to serve God and to be with Jesus as he carried his cross. Whatever the details of the experience, Ignatius understood it to be on the one hand a confirmation of the past: that God had been leading him and his friends up to that point. But it was also an opening to the future. Whatever happened to them in Rome, this experience indicated that their vocation was in some sense to be 'placed with the Son' in his mission and in his death and resurrection. Later on, when they came to discuss their future more fully in Rome, Ignatius and his friends allowed this incident to influence the shape and mission of the Society of Jesus that they founded.

The main inspiration of Ignatius's work among people was still his personal devotion to Jesus, which had been born all those years ago at Loyola. As time went on this had broadened out into a deeper awareness of and concern for the Church which Jesus founded. The aim which Ignatius and his companions had in deciding to go to Rome was to offer themselves to the pope to be at the service of the Church. This was not an arbitrary decision but a consequence of their devotion to Jesus. They wanted to 'serve the Lord alone and his spouse the Church' and for them the pope was the representative of Jesus at the head of the Church. By offering and binding themselves to the pope, to accept the missions that he asked of them, they would be fulfilling the commitment to follow and imitate

Jesus which each of them had first made in the Second and following Weeks of the Spiritual Exercises (Exx 98, 147, 234).

From 1539 to 1556 when Ignatius was head of the growing Society of Jesus in Rome the form of his own involvement in the work of evangelizing and 'helping souls' changed considerably. He continued to give the Exercises occasionally in Rome and places nearby. He reached people by writing letters in which he offered help and guidance in friendship to a large number. He also helped to establish in Rome a 'house of catechumens', an orphanage and refuge for prostitutes. But his main task became that of enabling the members of the new order to continue and expand their mission and of establishing structures by which that could continue.

This task had several different aspects. It was first of all a matter of deciding where to send his men so that they might be most effective in serving the Church and the people most in need of the help they could give. He received a growing number of requests for Jesuits to be sent to different places throughout Europe and the wider world and, as he had a limited number of men at his disposal, he had to decide how best to respond. It was out of the experience of having to make these choices that he was able to formulate his 'criteria for choice of ministries' which offer principles and guidelines for making decisions about which missions and ministries to choose.[20] At the same time Ignatius also kept in touch by letter with as many as possible of the Jesuits scattered through the world. He offered them encouragement and guidance on how they were to carry out their missions. And a very important aspect of his indirect evangelizing work was, of course, the composition of the *Constitutions* of the new Society. By putting into writing the principles and structures by which the Society could become a permanent body of men with a distinctive spirit and style of life, he offered to his own and future generations of Jesuits the opportunity to carry out their missions corporately, strengthened and supported by their union with one another.

Personal experience

Though necessarily sketchy, the images of Ignatius that we have looked at have enabled us to understand him more fully and to explore different aspects of his personality. They have also enabled us to see some patterns of change and growth which took place in him in the course of time. I want to end with a few reflections.

It is clear from Ignatius's autobiography that experience was the main catalyst of change in his life. Ignatius's spiritual growth was not a matter of first having a theory and then trying to bring his practice into line with the theory, even though to some degree that was how he started out after his conversion: by taking the saints as models and trying to shape his life according to those models. But that did not last long. The time he spent at Manresa seems to have shown him that God was present and at work in his own experience, in the events of his own life. So the pattern of growing which he developed was not based on imitation of outstanding examples of discipleship. Rather he noted the main features of his own experiences and, reflecting on them, saw in them the signs of God's presence and action. The consequent decisions that he made about what his next step should be were based on this reflection. A clear example of that is his decision to study in order to be able to 'help souls', which arose from his pilgrimage and Jerusalem experience. His own experience, appropriated reflectively, provided him with pointers as to what he should do next. And similarly in 1538 when Ignatius and his companions were trying to give shape to their future, they reflected on their individual and collective experience up to that point and found there pointers as to the direction their lives should take.[21] That pattern of reflecting on one's own experience, appreciating the gifts received and using them as pointers to the direction in which God is leading was a fundamental pattern for growth in the lives of Ignatius and his companions.

This leads to another reflection which is crucial for our understanding of Ignatian spirituality in the circumstances of our own time. If we are to enter more fully into Ignatius's way of being a disciple of Jesus, this does not mean finding out what Ignatius thought and did and imitating that literally and simplistically; as if merely saying, 'Ignatius did this, therefore I must do it'. On the other hand what Ignatius said and did in particular circumstances is by no means irrelevant to us. For Jesuits in particular, careful pondering of his words and actions is a very important element in continuing discernment. Ignatius's experience and practice act as an inspiration and guide to us. At the same time Ignatian spirituality also leads us to note and reflect on our own personal and communal experience; believing that God is and has been present in that story, those years of 'living and partly living'; appreciating the gifts of God in that history, and yet at the same time finding matter for sorrow there; praising the giver for the gifts, and, when we are faced with a crucial fork in the road, using these intimations of God's faithfulness to help us determine the path we should take. Both our own story, in the ecclesial and social context in which that story is lived, and our reflections on what Ignatius said and did are essential elements in our discernments today.[22]

1   I have already mentioned the value and limitations of Ignatius's Autobiography. The standard accounts of Ignatius and the early Jesuits available in English include the following: James Brodrick SJ, *The origin of the Jesuits* (Longmans, Green, London, 1940); *The progress of the Jesuits* (Longmans, Green, London, 1946); *Saint Ignatius Loyola: the pilgrim years* (Burns and Oates, London, 1956); Paul Dudon SJ, *Saint Ignatius of Loyola*, tr. William J. Young SJ (Bruce Publishing, Milwaukee, 1949); Mary Purcell, *The first Jesuit* (Loyola University Press, Chicago, 1981); Georg Schurhammer SJ, *Francis Xavier: his life, his times*, vol. 1, *Europe (1506–1541)*, tr. Joseph M. Costelloe SJ (Jesuit Historical Institute, Rome, 1973); Candido de Dalmases SJ, *Ignatius of Loyola, founder of the Jesuits: his life and work*, tr. Jerome Aixala SJ (Institute of Jesuit Sources, St Louis 1985); André Ravier SJ. *Ignatius of Loyola and the founding of the Society of Jesus*, tr. Maura Daly, Joan Daly and Carson Daly (Ignatius Press, San Francisco, 1987); Joseph de Guibert SJ, *The Jesuits, their spiritual doctrine and practice: a historical study*, tr. William J. Young SJ (Institute of Jesuit Sources/Loyola University Press, Chicago, 1964).
2   The likeness to Don Quixote has not gone unnoticed: cf. Paul Edwards SJ, 'Loyola and La Mancha', *The Way Supplement* 55 (Spring 1986), pp. 3–15.

3   For a fuller treatment of the feudal and literary influences upon Ignatius's image of Jesus, see Robert L. Schmitt, 'The Christ-experience and relationship fostered in the Spiritual Exercises of Ignatius Loyola', *Studies in the Spirituality of Jesuits*, vol. VI, no. 5 (October 1974).

4   Formula of the Institute [3], in *Constitutions*, p. 66.

5   cf. Schmitt, op. cit.

6   See also Autobiography, 15–16. One of Ignatius's own brothers set out for America and died in Darien (Dalmases, op. cit. p. 14).

7   Many of Ignatius's letters to a wide range of people are full of affection and friendship. See for example *Letters of Ignatius Loyola*, sel. and tr. William J. Young SJ (Loyola University Press, Chicago, 1959), pp. 18–24, 24–5, 83–6, 214–18, 244, 257–8, 316–17, 323–4, 328–30, 336–7, 347–9, 355–6, 358, 402, 405–6.

8   cf. Jules J. Toner SJ, 'The deliberation that started the Jesuits', *Studies in the Spirituality of Jesuits*, vol. VI, no. 4, p. 192.

9   cf. *Constitutions*, 673–6, 790; *Letters*, pp. 62–4.

10 Autobiography, 9, 14, etc.; *General Examen*, 101–2, in *Constitutions*, pp. 108–9.

11 André Ravier attributes most of the flaws in the Church of the time to benefices and their misuse: cf. André Ravier, *Ignatius of Loyola and the founding of the Society of Jesus* (Ignatius Press, San Francisco, 1987), ch. 2.

12 It is ironic that, having avoided the path of a career cleric, Ignatius in fact became one of the more influential clerics in Rome in his time.

13 In their final profession, professed Jesuits promise not to seek positions of power and authority in the Society or the church.

14 Ignatius wanted the Society to practise a mendicant poverty, as far as that is possible for a body of people with responsibility for training and supporting its own members and for maintaining institutions such as churches, schools, colleges and universities.

15 Ignatius's account of his adventures in Jerusalem is in Autobiography, 45–8.

16 cf. Autobiography, 22–6.

17 This was the desire with which he frequently ended his letters: 'that God will give us the grace to know his most holy will and to carry it out'.

18 cf. *General Examen*, 67, in *Constitutions*, p. 97.

19 *Constitutions*, pt VII; cf. also Joseph Veale, 'Ignatian criteria for choice of ministries', *The Way Supplement* 55 (Spring 1986), pp. 77–88.

20 cf. *Constitutions*, pt VII.

21 cf. Jules J. Toner, op. cit.

22 Pierre Favre, who was a companion of Ignatius from Paris days, a master of discernment of spirits and who is said to have been, among the first companions, the best giver of the Exercises, began his own

spiritual journal with a thanksgiving verse from Ps. 103 and an account of what he saw as the main gifts and blessings in his life and experience up to that point: cf. Bienhereux Pierre Favre, *Memorial*, tr. and ed. Michel de Certeau SJ (Desclée de Brouwer, Paris, 1960), pp. 105ff.

2

IGNATIUS AND JESUS

Ignatius's interest in theology was not an interest in theological knowledge for its own sake. He went to study, as we have seen, in order to be able to 'help souls'. And it has to be admitted that he never showed any great aptitude for the kind of abstract systematic thought that characterized academic theology at that time. He was far more at home with images, stories and pictures than with more abstract concepts. It is characteristic of him, for example, that in the meditations on sin in the First Week of the Exercises what he offers is not a theological discussion of sin but the story of sin in human experience as told in scripture (Exx 45–54). And when he recommends in the Second Week that those making the Exercises should contemplate the mystery of the incarnation, he presents that in the form of a story made up of a series of pictures or tableaux (Exx 101–9). This natural penchant for images, pictures and stories, which are of course no less theologically respectable than abstract concepts, is also one reason why he is so much at home with scripture.

To say that Ignatius was no speculative theologian however is not to say, obviously, that he was not interested in knowledge of God, which is what theology is. On the contrary it was knowledge of God that made such a radical difference in his own life. Both for himself and for others he looked for the kind of knowledge of God that gives rise to love and to a closer discipleship of Jesus; the knowledge of God, therefore, that answers people's deepest aspirations, moves their affections and influences their choices and commitments. Because he wanted to help others to experience God for themselves he put some of his own experience of God into the *Spiritual Exercises* as an aid for other people to use.

When we examine Ignatius's images of Jesus and God therefore we are not primarily looking for sparkle or originality in his discussion or development of theological ideas. (Most of the book of the *Spiritual Exercises* makes very dull reading; perhaps the dullest is the part where Ignatius attempts a more academic type of theology, as in sections 32–42, on different kinds of sin.) We are looking rather at the basic images of God and Jesus that held greatest significance for him. Like the rest of us, he took these images somewhat eclectically from scripture, the books he read, the people he met, the world in which he lived and his own inner experience. Their significance is not their theological originality but their apparent power to make a difference to the actual life of Ignatius. We are looking at the images which had a significant influence on his choices, his commitments and consequently on the shape of his life.

The importance of images of Jesus and God

Our images of God are the usual, habitual ways that we have of thinking about God, imagining God and referring to God in words, gestures, music, pictures or other forms of expression. They are the forms in which we represent God either inwardly for ourselves or externally to others. These images, like the images that we have of other realities such as ourselves and the world in which we live, have a powerful influence on our behaviour. Our images of ourselves, of Jesus and of God, for example, help to give shape to our lives as Christians. If the dominant image that I have of God is that of some kind of taskmaster, I will tend to see my Christian life largely as a series of tasks or duties to be performed in order to satisfy the God who sets these tasks and who demands them to be carried out, so we imagine, in a certain way and according to high standards of achievement. Many people do try to live as Christians under the dominance of images of this kind and not surprisingly often feel burdened and oppressed. On the other hand people for whom God is predominantly like, for example, the father in Jesus's story of the prodigal son, experience and live Christianity very differently: with more gratitude and love and correspondingly less fear.

Our images of ourselves and of God – and of ourselves in relation to God – also affect other images which are important for our Christian lives: images of what faith, sin and forgiveness are, for instance, or of what the Church and the sacraments are, and the ultimate realities of death and eternal life. If I tend to deal with God habitually as if God were like the father in the parable of the prodigal son, my images of sin and reconciliation will obviously be very different from those of another person who mainly sees God as a strict judge who applies 'the law' with some rigour.

All of our images are inadequate because God is always beyond what we can imagine. On the other hand they are valid because they are vital aids to knowing and to sustaining a living relationship with God. Our images of God, as of ourselves, can often be distorted however, and Christian growth frequently means discarding or correcting our more distorted images and taking up more adequate ones. But distorted or not, these images of God, like our fundamental images of ourselves and the world in which we live, exert a powerful and constant influence on our behaviour.

This influence is more often than not unconscious. We can be quite unaware both of the content of the inner images that affect us and of the fact that we are influenced in this way. It is often only when we reflect on what we believe, how we live and the attitudes which are revealed by our words and actions that we realize what the images are by which we are ruled. If it happens, for example, that I have a very lackadaisical, complacent approach to morality, it might become clear, if I take the trouble to reflect, that this approach is encouraged or even to a large degree determined by my habitual image of God as an indulgent father ready to smile at and approve easily whatever his spoilt children might do or fail to do. But it may be only when I reflect specifically on links between my behaviour and the forms in which I represent or address God that I become aware of the power of these images.

Even if we are not aware of the content of our images or of their influence in our lives and our behaviour, nevertheless they are still present and active, and their power is felt by others. It is now widely recognized, for instance, that the scarcity of feminine images of God in Christian culture has a direct bearing on the predominance of patriarchy in western society, and vice versa. Images of God affect not only the behaviour of individual people, but also social structures and institutions, which in turn affect individuals' or a group's favoured images.[1]

My reason for looking carefully at Ignatius's images of Jesus and God is that they significantly influenced his behaviour and thus form an integral part of his way of being a disciple of Christ. But our interest here is not just historical in the sense of wanting to know as fully as possible how, against the background of his own times, Ignatius imagined God and Jesus to be. We are looking at Ignatius as a man of the past, certainly, but also as one whose approach to Christian discipleship has something valuable to offer us here and now.

Images of Jesus

In a very real and practical sense Jesus was the way to God for Ignatius. It was through reading about Jesus in Ludolph of Saxony's *Life of Christ*, which he read during his convalescence at Loyola, that Ignatius discovered God and radically changed the direction of his life. Theology speaks about Jesus as mediator between God and humanity. Ignatius discovered this relationship in his experience before he ever came into contact with it in schools of theology. Ludolph of Saxony introduced him to Jesus and Jesus introduced him to God. He had 'known' God in some sense before Pamplona of course, as he had been brought up a Catholic and was mindful enough of Catholic practice to make his confession before going into battle (Autobiography, 1). But the God Ignatius met through Jesus during his convalescence was overwhelmingly new. In this chapter and the next we will highlight some of Ignatius's personal images of Jesus and of God.

Ignatius's strong attraction towards the person of Jesus seems to have begun during his convalescence, and at that time he expressed it in apparently naive and very tangible forms. He took with him on his pilgrimage a notebook in which he had copied out passages from the gospels, with the words of Jesus emphasized in red ink

(Autobiography, 11). His hope in going to Jerusalem was to be able to see and touch the places where Jesus had been, and in his Autobiography he wrote of the feelings that he experienced as he visited the holy places (Autobiography, 45). In Jerusalem he twice successfully bribed the guards to let him visit Mount Olivet. The second time was because he had forgotten to notice the direction in which the imprints of the feet of Jesus were facing in the stone from which he ascended into heaven (Autobiography, 47). At that time his was the kind of devotion that feeds on such details and on this tangible contact with the places associated with Jesus. Jesus was constantly the object of his contemplation.

Though his attachment to Jesus became less naive with time, it remained a powerful inspiration and shaper of his activity to the end of his life. He was adamant that the religious order he founded should have no other name than that of Jesus.

Underlying Ignatius's devotion to the historical Jesus of course there is the traditional Christian belief that Jesus was and is the Son of God, the Word made flesh. For Ignatius Jesus was the one who had come from the side of God to redeem fallen, sinful humanity (cf. Exx 101–9). Jesus was both divine and human. So we find Ignatius saying that in the passion and death of Jesus the divinity 'hides itself' (Exx 196), and the fragile humanity is clearly seen. In the gospel resurrection stories by contrast we can see 'the divinity now appearing and manifesting itself so miraculously . . . in its true and most sacred effects' (Exx 223). This belief in Jesus as the Son of God, the second person of the Trinity incarnate, allows Ignatius to refer to Jesus with titles such as 'our Creator and Lord' and 'the Divine Majesty'.

We have seen in Chapter 1 how Ignatius's understanding of his following of Jesus was greatly influenced by ideals enshrined in the romances that he read and by his own experience of being a soldier, with his idealized notions of honour and glory. This influence is especially reflected in the *Spiritual Exercises*. It is unlikely that the historical Jesus thought of or referred to himself in terms of kingship. The gospels present him to us as correcting and even repudiating the glory and political power associated with the title of 'Christ' in the minds of the people around him (Mark 8:27–38; John 6:15;

18:36–40). None the less in the *Spiritual Exercises* Ignatius brings before us Jesus as a king who is also a 'knight companion', inviting others to join him in his enterprise 'to conquer the whole world and all my enemies, and thus to enter into the glory of my Father' (Exx 95). In the meditations on the Call of the King and the Two Standards Jesus explains further the aims of the enterprise, the conditions of service and the methods by which he will come to victory:

> Therefore whoever wishes to join me in this enterprise must be willing to labour with me, that by following me in suffering, he or she may follow me in glory. (Exx 95)

> . . . the Lord of all the world chooses so many persons, apostles, disciples etc., and sends them throughout the whole world to spread his sacred doctrine among all people, no matter what their state or condition. (Exx 145)

So one of the main images of Jesus in the *Exercises* is that of the 'Lord of all the world' who invites others to join him in conquering the whole world for his Father by helping to spread his teaching among all nations. He offers companionship, a share in a worthwhile and even noble enterprise which calls for daring and generosity, with the hope of honour and glory. Ignatius's language is military in the terms of his own age, but it is also the language of personal appeal and response. The king is a man of superior standing, but also a friend who offers an invitation which Ignatius thinks any right-minded person could not resist. It is typical of Ignatius too, with his ideals of honour and glory, that he envisages the possibility of a more generous and enthusiastic response:

> Those who wish to give greater proof of their love and to distinguish themselves in whatever concerns the service of the Eternal King and Lord of all, will not only offer themselves entirely for the work, but will act against their sensuality and carnal and worldly love, and make offerings of greater value and of more importance . . . (Exx 97)

An image of Jesus which dominates the *Exercises* even more is that of Jesus the evangelizer whose mission leads ultimately to his death and resurrection, an image to which Ignatius was also powerfully drawn. In the Second Week Ignatius selects incidents from the gospels which provide the material for contemplation for those who are making the Exercises. The section on the Call of the King introduces this Second Week, and it is interesting that the emphasis on Jesus's travelling mission of the word appears immediately here: 'see in imagination the synagogues, towns and villages where Christ our lord preached' (Exx 91). This sets the pattern for the whole of the Second Week, for it also dominates Ignatius's choice of incidents from the gospels which are to be included in the Second Week and his choice of the supplementary mysteries of the life of Jesus which the one who makes the Exercises is also invited to use (Exx 261–88). Hence in the Second Week of the Exercises Ignatius ignores almost entirely the miracles of Jesus and focuses on his mission of preaching and teaching. 'Ignatius, in the body of the Spiritual Exercises proposes no miracle as a contemplative exercise and, of the fifty-two appended meditations on the life of Jesus, only five are miracles and none of these is a healing or exorcism.'[2]

This underlining of the fact that Jesus was a man with a mission among people and that this mission was mainly a matter of preaching and teaching is a clear sign that both of these were important to Ignatius himself. The conditions of the Church in Europe in Ignatius's own time partly account for this emphasis. He was struck by the widespread ignorance of the teaching of Jesus and of basic Christian doctrine among the clergy and people, a condition which the Council of Trent recognized and tried to remedy. And this emphasis is also reflected in his ideas about the kind of ministry that Jesuits might be involved in. He gave a high priority to preaching and teaching, especially teaching Christian doctrine to children and uneducated people, which led him to devote much time and energy later to establishing colleges. He described the order as:

a Society founded chiefly for this purpose: to strive especially for the defense and propagation of the faith and for the progress of souls in Christian life and doctrine, by means of public preaching, lectures and any other ministration whatsoever of the word of God, and further by means of the Spiritual Exercises, the education of children and unlettered persons in Christianity, and the spiritual consolation of Christ's faithful through hearing confessions and administering the other sacraments.[3]

Another characteristic feature of Ignatius's image of Jesus is an emphasis on Jesus's poverty. Here again the conditions in which Ignatius lived probably account at least in part for this emphasis. He held that one of the roots of abuse and corruption in the Church at the time was the pursuit of wealth, especially among the clergy. His own choice and experience of poverty as a pilgrim and poor student also obviously influenced his attitudes profoundly. In addition during his studies he and his companions had had contact with Franciscans and admired their ideal. And his experience at La Storta on the way to Rome also no doubt affected his later choice of poverty for himself and the Society. When he felt that the Father 'placed' him with the Son, the image of the Son that he 'saw' was not the risen Lord in glory but Jesus carrying his cross: Jesus the servant in poverty.

The poverty of Jesus, which Ignatius offers for imitation so emphatically, has several dimensions. One of the features of the whole mystery of the incarnation and the life, death and resurrection of Jesus which seems to have affected Ignatius profoundly is its gratuitous nature. Without any necessity, but purely out of love for humanity, the Son of God came into the world so that the world might be saved. As Ignatius saw it (much in the spirit of Phil. 2:1–11), this involved the Word of God in a self-emptying: both in taking on the human condition and, within that, in accepting a life which involved humiliation, hardship, labour, suffering and a painful and degrading death; and all this out of love for ungrateful and faithless humanity. Ignatius applied this to himself and to others in a very personal way; looking at what Christ has done for *me* out of love:

Imagine Christ our Lord present before you on the cross, and begin to speak with him, asking how it is that though he is the

Creator, he has stooped to become human and to pass from eternal life to death here in time, that thus he might die for our sins. (Exx 53)

Later on the person who is making the Exercises is asked to look at Mary and Joseph at the time of Jesus's birth and 'consider what they are doing, for example, making the journey and labouring that our Lord might be born in extreme poverty, and that after many labours, after hunger, thirst, heat and cold, after insults and outrages, he might die on the cross, and all this for me' (Exx 116). This way of looking at the mystery of Jesus, with its underlying theology of self-emptying, is not unusual in the theological and devotional writing of Ignatius's time.[4] It reappears at greater length in some of Ignatius's later letters. In 1547 he wrote to a group of Jesuits stressing the price paid by Jesus for our salvation as an encouragement to love in return:

But more than anything else I should wish to awaken in you the pure love of Jesus Christ, the desire for his honour and for the salvation of souls whom he has redeemed. For you are his soldiers in this society with a special title and a special wage ... His wage is everything you are in the natural order ... His wage is also the spiritual gifts of his grace with which he has so generously and lovingly anticipated you ... His wage is also those incomparable blessings of his glory which, without any advantage to himself, he ... holds in readiness for you ... Finally his wage is the whole universe and everything material and spiritual it contains ... As though this wage were not enough, he has made himself our wage, becoming a brother in our own flesh, as the price of our salvation on the cross and in the Eucharist to be with us as support and company ... We know indeed that to oblige us to desire and labour for this glory, his majesty has anticipated us with these inestimable and priceless favours, in a sense stripping himself of his own possessions to give us a share in them; taking upon himself all our miseries to deliver us from them; wishing to be sold as our redemption, to be dishonoured to glorify us, to be poor to enrich us; accepting a disgraceful and painful death to give us a blessed and immortal life . . . How extremely ungrateful and hardhearted is he who after all this does not recognize his obligation to serve our Lord Jesus Christ diligently and to seek his honour.[5]

Poverty then, for Jesus, was not so much a matter of arbitrary choice (still less of enforced destitution) as a consequence and a sign of who he was and of his wholehearted fidelity to his mission. He represented God and the values of God in a world largely dominated by self-seeking and the self-interested exercise of power. As a result he identified himself with all human beings in their poverty and fragility, including the lowest and most rejected. He rejected the pursuit of wealth and power which goes with ambition and self-interest, and instead offered himself freely and generously in love for the service and healing of others. Because he was wholly faithful to his mission for others, he was content to live as a poor man. And because his faithfulness to his mission and to what he saw as God's values led him into conflict with people in positions of power, he had to suffer humiliation, insult and finally death at their hands. He accepted this way because to do otherwise would have been a betrayal of God, the people he served and himself. These features of Jesus's mission are summed up in what Ignatius calls poverty.

It is worth noting too that for Ignatius the poverty of Jesus is also, paradoxically, his way of being the 'Eternal King' and 'Lord of all the world'. This paradox lies at the heart of the mystery of Jesus and re-echoes the discussions in the gospels about the kind of Messiah Jesus is. Whereas ordinarily, in Ignatius's experience, kings and lords are surrounded with wealth and its symbols, exercise the power that goes with it and will not tolerate humiliation and insult, Jesus's kingship takes another form, 'not of this world' (John 18:36); the form of the servant who takes the way of poverty. The followers of Jesus are presented then with a stark choice between two sets of values and attitudes. Ignatius recommends that candidates who want to join the Society should be shown clearly:

to how great a degree it helps and profits one in the spiritual life to abhor in its totality and not in part whatever the world loves and embraces, and to accept and desire with all possible energy whatever Christ our Lord has loved and embraced. Just as the men of the world . . . love and seek with such great diligence honours, fame and esteem for a great name on earth . . . so those who are progressing in the spiritual life and truly following Christ our Lord love and intensely desire everything opposite. That is to say they desire to clothe themselves with the same clothing and uniform of their Lord because of the love and reverence which he deserves, to such an extent that where there would be no offence to his Divine Majesty and no imputation of sin to the neighbour, they would wish to suffer injuries, false accusations and affronts, and to be held and esteemed as fools (but without their giving any occasion for this) because of their desire to resemble and imitate in some manner our Creator and Lord Jesus Christ, by putting on his clothing and uniform, since it was for our spiritual profit that he clothed himself as he did. For he gave us an example that in all things possible to us we might seek . . . to imitate and follow him, since he is the way which leads men to life.[6]

A crowd of shadows seem to hover at Ignatius's shoulder as he writes this: the Medicis, Borgias, Gonzagas and others of that ilk in their power and splendour; kings, popes, cardinals and even the career cleric that he himself did not become.

In the Second and Third Weeks of the Spiritual Exercises the image of Jesus which Ignatius presents for daily contemplation is that of the man who is also the Son of God and who pursues his evangelizing mission in poverty till it leads ultimately to his death on the cross. In the Fourth Week, where the focus is on the risen Jesus, the image is slightly different. As the risen Lord, of course, Christ is implicitly present in the whole process of the Exercises. By his presence in the Church and in the lives of those who make the Exercises, he is with his disciples always, even to the end of time, as he promised. The image that the Fourth Week offers however is not that of the wandering preacher of the word, but Jesus the friend and consoler (Exx 224). It is as friend and consoler that his disciples meet him in the gospel resurrection stories; and it is as friend and consoler therefore that he meets his disciples 'to the end of time'. This image represents another dimension of the presence and activity of the risen Lord in the Church and it is the image of Jesus with which the Exercises end.

Jesus as the Son of God has a special place in Ignatius's own prayer and in the prayer that he recommends to people who are making the Exercises. He sees 'the Son' as an intermediary between the person who prays and God who is the Father. The link with Ignatius's own experience provides the setting for seeing the Son in this role. Ignatius liked to imagine God as a king, the Divine Majesty, surrounded by the 'whole court of heaven' (Exx 74, 98, 106). The person who prays, then, is like a petitioner at that court, an ordinary person who wishes to communicate with the Divine Majesty, in order to praise, to offer thanks, to express sorrow, to petition and so on. The Son of God is one of the people – along with his mother and other saints – whom we call upon as an intermediary with God, an intercessor who will act on our behalf with the 'Divine Majesty'.

This image of the Son, whom he also sometimes refers to in this context as 'the Word incarnate' was very significant for Ignatius. From the First Week onwards in the Exercises he recommends that the exercitants should end each session of prayer with what he calls a 'colloquy'. Ignatius recommends that when we are in need of a particular gift we should first ask Our Lady to obtain it for us from her Son; then the Son to obtain it for us from the Father; then we should ask the Father himself (Exx 63, 147, 148 etc.). Ignatius's Spiritual Journal shows that he found this framework of prayer, and the image of the Son as intermediary, helpful in his own contemplation even as late as 1554.[7]

We have looked at Ignatius's images of Jesus as 'Eternal King' who is also a 'knight-companion', as travelling preacher and teacher, as a man who espoused poverty, as a friend and consoler and as an intermediary at the court of the Divine Majesty. We have also explored some of their meanings, though not exhaustively, because these images are symbols and they embody many meanings. They have their roots in scripture and Christian traditions of theology and spirituality, either immediately or more remotely. And Ignatius has married images from scripture and the traditions with images – not necessarily religious ones – from his own experience in a process of assimilating, adapting and developing.

1 For further discussion of the importance and power of such images see, for example, Kathleen R. Fischer, *The inner rainbow: the imagination in Christian life* (Paulist Press, New York, 1983), esp. chs 1,4,5,6. On the discussion of Ignatius's own images in this chapter and the next, see Joseph Thomas SJ., *Le Christ de Dieu pour Ignace de Loyola* (Desclée, Paris, 1981).

2 John R. Donahue, 'Miracle, mystery and parable', *The Way*, vol. 18, no. 4 (October 1978), p. 252.

3 *The Formula of the Institute*, s. 3, in *Constitutions*, p. 66.

4 The article by P. Henry, 'Kénose' in *Dictionnaire de la Bible: Supplement*, contains a masterly historical survey of this topic.

5 *Letters*, pp. 124–5; cf. also pp. 146–50.

6 *General Examen*, s. 101 in *Constitutions*, pp. 107–8.

7 On 25 February 1544, for example, Ignatius wrote: 'During the prayers to the Father, it seemed that Jesus was presenting them, or accompanied those that I was saying before the Father', *Inigo: discernment log-book. The Spiritual Diary of Saint Ignatius Loyola*, ed. and tr. Joseph A. Munitiz SJ (Inigo Enterprises, London, 1987), s. 77. Cited as *Spiritual Diary*.

3

THE WORLD AND THE TRINITY

The Trinity

He had a great devotion to the Most Holy Trinity, and thus daily
prayed to the Three Persons distinctly . . . One day, while he was
reciting the Hours of Our Lady on the steps of the same monastery, his understanding began to be elevated, as though he saw
the Holy Trinity under the figure of three keys. This was
accompanied with so many tears and so much sobbing that he
could not control himself . . . and was not able to restrain his
tears until dinner time. Nor afterwards could he stop talking
about the Most Holy Trinity. He made use of many different
comparisons, and experienced great joy and consolation. The
result was that all through his life this great impression has
remained with him, to feel great devotion when he prays to the
Most Holy Trinity. (Autobiography, 28)

This incident happened at a monastery near Manresa early in
Ignatius's pilgrimage. As a result of it the Trinity became a source
of inspiration to him both in his prayer and, flowing from that, in
his work of 'helping souls'. Once again it is characteristic of him
(and perhaps disappointing to us) that his description of the content
of the experience is so meagre: 'under the figure of three keys'
(*teclas*). But whatever the content the total impact was obviously
powerful and long-lasting.

Modern theology draws a distinction between the 'economic' and
the 'immanent' Trinity. Discussion of the immanent Trinity focuses
on relationships between the 'persons' of the triune God within the
Godhead; whereas to talk about the economic Trinity is to pay

attention to the creative and saving work of God in the world and in history, that is, in the 'economy' of salvation. As we have already seen, Ignatius is not a speculative theologian, so it is not altogether surprising that his images of the Trinity are concerned with the 'economic' aspects: God's dealings with men and women in history in the world which they inhabit.

Ignatius sets out his basic understanding of the work of the Trinity in the contemplation on the incarnation at the start of the Second Week of the *Spiritual Exercises*. His aim is a practical one at this point: to offer material for contemplation, so that the person who does the exercise may have 'an intimate knowledge of our Lord, who has become incarnate for me, that I may love him more and follow him more closely' (Exx 104). So first he provides a summary of the story: 'the three Divine Persons look down upon the whole expanse or circuit of the earth filled with human beings . . . They decree in their eternity that the Second Person should become incarnate to save the human race' (Exx 102). The contemplation's main structure is a comparison and contrast between three different pictures: the whole earth and its people, the 'three Divine Persons' and the Annunciation scene with Mary and the angel. The comparison hinges on the 'persons' themselves, what they are saying and what they are doing.

This contemplation gives us a narrative and pictorial image of how Ignatius understood the Trinity. In contrast to the variety and bustle of people 'on the face of the earth', we are asked to look at: 'the Three Divine Persons seated on the royal dais or throne of the Divine Majesty. They look down upon the whole surface of the earth, and behold all nations in great blindness, going down to death and descending into hell' (Exx 106). Then in contrast to hear 'what the persons on the face of the earth say . . . how they speak to one another, swear and blaspheme, etc.', 'I will also hear what the Divine Persons say, that is, "Let us work the redemption of the human race"' (Exx 107). Finally we are asked to consider 'what the persons on the face of the earth do, for example, wound, kill and go down to hell', whereas 'what the Divine Persons do' is 'work the most holy Incarnation' (Exx 108).

These few words give us the essentials of Ignatius's basic image of the Trinity. There is a sharp contrast between the confusion on earth and the royal throne of the 'Divine Majesty'; between the powerlessness of the people on earth to help themselves, trapped in their own destructiveness, and the power of God; and between the evil on earth and the goodness of the 'three Divine Persons' whose attention is wholly directed towards acting for the good of the troubled men and women whom they see in the world.

This contemplation also reflects the traditional Christian view that from the time of the fall of Adam and Eve until the death of Jesus humanity was wholly 'ungraced' and incapable of coming to salvation. The fact that the world was seen as deprived of grace accounts for the pessimistic view of human life before the coming of Christ which is contained in Ignatius's meditation. This represents Ignatius's view of humanity when unable to be touched by grace. All on the face of the earth are locked in self-destructive behaviour which takes them 'down to hell' and they are unable to set themselves free. The gratuitous decree of the 'Divine Persons' to save the human race is an act of sheer goodness, and universal in its scope. But it is worthwhile noting that Ignatius offers no theological explanation as to why, for instance, the redemption of humanity implies the incarnation of the 'Second Person' of the Trinity. The story itself in an accessible form, rather than a discussion of its underlying theology, is his main interest.

For Ignatius the link between the Trinity and his own mission was fairly obvious and straightforward. God sent his Son into the world so that the world might be saved. That mission of the Son continues in every age, and the Son invites men and women to join him in this mission. When Ignatius and his companions offered themselves to the pope for the service of the Church, they saw this as a public sign of wanting to be companions and collaborators with Jesus and the Trinity.

We can see from Ignatius's Spiritual Journal how images of the Trinity came into his own prayer. The journal is partly a record of what happened during his prayer at the time when he was writing the *Constitutions* and trying to decide what form of poverty would be appropriate to the Society of Jesus as a whole. Again the basic image seems to be that Ignatius sees himself as a petitioner who needs to 'find favour' at the royal court of the 'Divine Majesty'. He hopes that God will 'confirm' the choice of poverty that he has made. The Son again acts as his mediator and intercessor. As for himself, Ignatius feels that the quality that he needs in order to approach the Trinity in his prayer is reverence. At one point in the journal he becomes distracted and irritated by some noise in the next room, and as a result feels temporarily shut off from the presence of the Trinity, though still able to approach by way of his 'mediators'. This privileged insight into Ignatius's personal prayer also illustrates the fact that there is consistency and continuity between the Exercises and his own contemplation, and that images of God from his early days endure into his later life.[1]

Occasionally in Ignatius's later letters and the *Constitutions* we catch glimpses of another kind of image of the Trinity: not this time the royal throne of heaven but people as images of the Trinity. To the Jesuits at Coimbra in 1547, in the course of a long letter on their mission and ministry, he wrote:

Can you find a place where the Divine Majesty is in honour today, or where his infinite greatness is worshipped, where his wisdom and infinite goodness are known or his most holy will obeyed? Behold rather, with deep grief, how his holy name is everywhere ignored, despised, blasphemed. The teaching of Jesus Christ is cast off, his example forgotten, and the price of his blood lost in a certain sense as far as we are concerned because there are so few to profit by it. Behold likewise your neighbours, images of the most holy Trinity and capable of enjoying his glory whom all the world serves, members of Christ, redeemed by so much pain, opprobrium, and blood. Behold, I say, the miseries that surround them, the darkness of ignorance that envelops them, and the whirlwind of desires, empty fears and other passions that torment them . . .[2]

And when, on instructions from Ignatius, Polanco was writing to another Jesuit in May 1556 he advised him that in his apostolic work he should see the people he was dealing with not as handsome or ugly but as 'the image of the most holy Trinity, as a member of Christ and bathed in his blood'.[3]

These phrases give us an interesting insight into how Ignatius's mind sometimes worked. We know that in general he was very aware of the presence and action of God in the world (cf. Exx 230–7). As his relationship with God deepened, created reality reminded him increasingly of God and drew him towards God, because in contemplating the gifts he was led back to the giver. Here it seems that his ability to see people as images of the Trinity helped to determine his attitude towards them and his treatment of them. The reverence that he felt in his prayer, for example, in the presence of the Trinity would flow into an attitude of reverence for people when he saw them as images of the Trinity.

Images of the Father

We find references to God as Father in two quite separate settings in Ignatius's writings. One is the context of prayer to the persons of the Trinity, and in this connection we have already seen how Ignatius liked to approach the Father through the mediation of the Son as well as praying to the Father and Holy Spirit directly. The other setting is in his letters, particularly later letters of comfort or condolence.

Ignatius is not concerned to be especially accurate in the way he applies different titles to God. He refers to both the Father and Jesus, for example, as 'the Divine Majesty' at different times. There are also occasions on which he seems to apply the title to the Godhead or Trinity without distinguishing different 'persons'. But in Ignatius's mind the Father seems to be the most remote of the persons of the Trinity, and thus the one who most represents the 'Divine Majesty', like a great king who lives apart. In his journal he records that he felt the Son was 'disposed to intercede with the Father', while at another time he felt he had 'free access to the Father'.[4]

The Father however is the ultimate source of authority and guidance for Ignatius in the decisions that he makes and the path that he follows. He told his companions that during the important experience which he had at La Storta on the way to Rome it was the Father who said to Jesus, 'I want this man to serve us', and who placed him, so Ignatius felt, 'with his Son'. And in his journal accounts of his prayer it is to the Father that he looks for confirmation and ratification of his choices.[5] Having come to a decision about poverty, he wrote: 'With great tranquillity and peace I made the election and the offering to the Father of not possessing anything even for the church.'[6]

Unlike his close friend Pierre Favre, Ignatius was not a *poète de l'esprit*.[7] Consequently we have no accurate or full descriptions of the content or nature of the images of the Father or the other 'persons' of the Trinity that Ignatius was aware of at such times. In any case he was always reticent about his own inner experience and was not writing a journal to be combed over 450 years later. It was only after considerable badgering that he could be prevailed upon to tell the story of his remarkable life. All we have are short phrases, such as when he records seeing 'in a certain way the being of the Father'. From hints such as these, however, we can gather some idea of the role that the person of the Father in the Trinity held for Ignatius in the context of his own prayer and apostolic life.

The other important setting in which Ignatius calls upon an image of the Father is in his later letters. We know of course that from 1548 onwards Ignatius employed Juan Polanco as his secretary, so that in the letters of the last eight years of his life we cannot be certain which images and expressions are those of Ignatius himself and which belong to Polanco. We can assume however that in general Polanco was a faithful scribe, as otherwise Ignatius was not the kind of man to have continued to employ him, and that the letters represent accurately the mind of Ignatius, even when they were not actually written by him in person. Here in any case we are not interested in the particular words that are used in the letters so much as the insight which the words give us into how Ignatius imaged God and related to God.

The letters in question are letters of comfort or condolence or support to people who are suffering illness, bereavement or pain caused by some other sorrowful or tragic event. For all of us these

experiences often raise questions about the goodness of God. They
show us that our experience of God has two aspects which often
seem contradictory. On the one hand we believe in and we sometimes feel in a tangible way the goodness and the love which God
has towards us. On the other hand times of suffering and affliction
make us question that goodness and love, while our pain seems to
show us a dark side of God that we do not like.

> Beyond saying sweet, past telling of tongue,
> Thou art lightning and love, I found it, a winter and warm.
> Father and fondler of heart thou hast wrung,
> Hast thy dark descending and most art merciful then.[8]

In his letters of comfort and support to people who are suffering
Ignatius often tries to help them to find some meaning in their
suffering by describing what he believes God is doing in such circumstances. His fundamental belief is that God is both wise and
good and that in all the situations that we find ourselves in and the
events that happen to us, even the most tragic, God is working for
our good. This, when stated baldly, may seem a very surprising
thing to say in the circumstances, and it is certainly not easy, nor
even possible sometimes for a person who is suffering intensely to
accept it. Ignatius uses three images of God in these contexts to
express his meaning: the images of providence, father and physician,
and one or two passages from his letters will give us a taste of what
these images meant to him.

Magdalene Angelica Domenech was the sister of a Jesuit. She
was suffering both from illness and from spiritual anxieties when
Ignatius wrote this to her in January 1554:

> Be persuaded that the divine and supreme goodness and love of
> our most wise Father in heaven is favouring you with that which
> will perfect you more, since in adversity no less than in prosperity,
> and in afflictions as well as in consolations, does he manifest the
> everlasting love with which he guides his chosen ones to eternal
> happiness.
>
> So great is his loving kindness, that, if it were good for us, he

would on his part be more inclined to keep us consoled rather than afflicted, even in this life. But as the condition of our misery in this present state requires that at times he visit us with trials instead of delights, we can see in this his fatherly and supreme mercy that he confines our trials to the brief course of this life and not without an occasional mingling of many consolations . . . If you try to put yourself into the hands of Christ our Lord by conforming your own will entirely with his, including a readiness to follow him in the trials he underwent in this world when he wishes to share them with you, so that you can follow him later in the glory of the other world, I have no doubt that your trials will cease in great measure . . .[9]

Mary Frassona del Gesso was a benefactress of the Society of Jesus who endowed a college in Ferrara. When she suffered from ill health and difficulties with her relatives, Ignatius again called on the images of God as providence, father and physician in trying to support her:

I have heard that your ladyship has been visited by God with a bodily infirmity as well as trials of soul, and I thought I should visit you by letter . . . and remind you (that) the providence of our most holy Father and wise Physician usually proceeds in this way with those whom he loves much . . .[10]

And in a letter to Father Francis de Attino, who was both ill and anxious, Ignatius told him that he should take all proper steps to get well:

Because all the sooner, then, with God's help, you will be freed from your illness to give yourself entirely to the service of God. And do not think that trying to recover your health is a slight occupation . . . As long as (God) visits you with illness, accept it as a very precious gift from the wisest and most affectionate of fathers and physicians. Be resolved especially both in mind and body, in work and in suffering, to be content with whatever pleases his divine providence.[11]

The mystery and paradox that we meet here are inherent in the Christian understanding of God's dealings with us. Ignatius clearly felt that the images of God as a 'wise and affectionate father' or 'the providence of our most holy father and wise physician' would help people to understand and accept more easily the unavoidable suffering which came to them. 'Providence', as a term connected with theological discussion rather than personal comfort, perhaps has associations which are abstract and impersonal. But the figure of a father 'whose hand is raised to strike as well as to caress'[12] resonates more warmly with the human experience of God in times of both joy and sorrow, without however destroying or solving the mystery.

The Holy Spirit

By this time the reader will not be surprised to learn that Ignatius had no developed or original theology of the Holy Spirit. In all of his writings the Holy Spirit is rarely mentioned explicitly. In fact, as we have seen, he ascribes to the risen Christ some of the roles that others might associate with the Spirit, such as being a friend or consoler (Exx 224). On the few occasions when he does refer to the Holy Spirit it is usually in the context of the Spirit's action in the lives of individual people. He attributes to the Spirit some of the roles that traditional Christian faith and theology have assigned to the Spirit. On the only occasion that he refers specifically to the Spirit in the *Spiritual Exercises* he states that the Spirit's role in the Church is to 'rule and govern', and that this is the same Spirit as the one who was active in the old dispensation in giving the commandments to the people of Israel (Exx 365). Similarly in the *Constitutions* the Spirit is said to 'write and engrave' upon our hearts 'the interior law of love and charity', to teach (414), to guide (624) and to inspire (624[k]).

In the context of his own discernment of spirits and decision-making however, Ignatius recorded in his journal some fragments of his own experience of the presence and work of the Spirit. On the days covered by the early part of his journal his practice was to celebrate the votive Mass of the Trinity and then afterwards pray about the decision he was making. Later he changed to celebrating the votive Mass of the Holy Spirit, and at that time the Spirit begins to figure more often in his journal. He describes the Spirit's role in his discernment:

> I prayed to Our Lady, then to the Son and to the Father that he might give me his spirit to assist me in my reasonings and to give me clarity of mind.[13]

> Later, with this same warmth I implored grace to reason with his spirit and to be moved by that spirit.[14]

Ignatius also felt at that time that the confirmation of his choices belonged in a special way to the Holy Spirit, as it did in the early Christian community.[15] But the mention in the same day's entry of a 'colloquy with the Holy Spirit' and pictorial images of the experience is unusual. The result is a felt confirmation of the decision he had taken:

> a little later I made a colloquy with the Holy Spirit in preparation for saying his Mass; I experienced the same devotion and tears and seemed to see or feel him in a dense clarity or in the colour of burning flame – a way quite strange with me – all of which confirmed me in my election.[16]

Like his other images of the 'persons' of the Trinity therefore, Ignatius's image of the Holy Spirit is very closely linked to his own experience. His concern was not to develop a fully-rounded theology of the Trinity but to allow the images of God that became significant in some way in his experience to influence his action. The image of the Spirit therefore helped him to move from prayer into practical choices, because he saw that his decision-making process was helped along at every stage by the presence and action of the Spirit. It is an image in which he perceives in a concrete way 'the Creator dealing with the creature and the creature with his Creator' (cf. Exx 15).

The world and God

There are two fundamental images in Ignatius's thinking and writing which provide us with a framework in which we can explore further his understanding of the interaction between God and the world, God and human history, God and individual men and women. The first is a picture in which he sees all good gifts of creation and salvation 'descending from above', 'as the rays of light descend from the sun, and as the waters flow from their fountains' (Exx 237). The second, which is obviously closely linked with this, is a perception of God as being present and active at all levels of created reality. And he expressed it in the language of the philosophical outlook of his time, which now might seem rather quaint, though we can see the point: 'in the elements giving them existence, in the plants giving them life, in the animals conferring upon them sensation, in humanity bestowing understanding' (Exx 235). We can begin to explore further Ignatius's view of God in relation to the world by looking more closely at these two images.

These two images form the foundation of the Contemplation to Attain Love in the *Spiritual Exercises*, where Ignatius asks the one who makes the exercise to look closely at the gifts he or she has received 'from above' and at signs of the presence of God in the world at large, and then in his or her own history. The purpose of the exercise is to engage the person who makes it in a movement of love towards God: appreciating the gifts of God to me and the constant, faithful, creative and saving presence of God in the world and in my own life I will be moved to respond by offering all I have to God in return (Exx 234).

Ignatius returns to this fundamental image again and again in different contexts, and a few brief quotations will show us how central an image it is. His view is that all of our lives and all that they contain are a gift from God, as is the whole universe in which we live. He illustrates it in the *Exercises* in this way: 'Thus my limited power comes from the supreme and infinite power above, and so too justice, goodness, mercy etc.' (Exx 237). In the *Constitutions* the image keeps recurring. He recommends, for instance, that his fellow Jesuits should try to accept even sickness 'as a gift from the hand of our Creator and Lord, since it is a gift no less than is health' (272). When he is trying to ensure that members of the Society will be united among themselves in 'the love of God our Lord', he maintains that this union will come about 'through that same love which will descend from the Divine Goodness and spread to all other men and women and particularly into the body of the Society' (671). Later on, setting out guidelines for reaching a decision in the General Congregation, the highest authoritative body within the Society, he returns to his metaphor of light: 'the light to perceive what can best be decided upon must come down from the First and Supreme Wisdom' (711; cf. 746). And when he is discussing the kind of person the Superior General should be, we find the fountain image again:

> the first (quality) is that he should be closely united with God our Lord and intimate with him in prayer and all his actions, that from God, the fountain of all good, the general may so much the better obtain for the whole body of the Society a large share of his gifts and graces . . . (723)

This leads quite naturally into our second image of God's involvement in the world as 'our Creator and Lord'. Ignatius's God is not at all a remote being who, as it were, created the universe on one occasion and after that left it to run and survive more or less on its own except for some occasional and quite specific divine interventions. If the world and history and all that is contained in them are gifts from the hand of God, then God is continuously present and engaged in created reality in every dimension of life and in a variety of different ways. God continues to create and sustain the universe and human history by being present there and participating. For Ignatius the whole created universe is the arena in which God continues to be both creator and saviour. And another very attractive image that Ignatius uses to express this is the image of God working hard on our behalf: 'consider how God works and labours for me in all creatures upon the face of the earth, that is, he conducts himself as one who labours' (Exx 236).

For Ignatius God's commitment to humanity and to the world,

which is expressed in the images we have been examining, is a commitment of love. It is because God loves the world that God pours out gifts upon it in plenty. Ignatius describes love in terms, not of romantic feeling but of a sharing of gifts (Exx 230–1). The gifts that God offers constantly to us are gifts and tokens of the love that governs all God's dealings with us: 'the lover gives and shares with the beloved what he possesses, or something of that which he has or is able to give; and vice versa, the beloved shares with the lover' (Exx 231). And Ignatius hopes that this pattern of God's dealings with us will evoke a like response of love in return:

> I will ponder with great affection how much God our Lord has done for me, and how much he has given me of what he possesses, and finally, how much, as far as he can, the same Lord desires to give himself to me according to his divine decrees.
>
> Then I will reflect upon myself and consider, according to all reason and justice, what I ought to offer the Divine Majesty, that is, all I possess and myself with it.

This response of love to love is the context in which Ignatius sets his now famous prayer: 'Take, Lord, and receive all my liberty, my memory, my understanding and my entire will, all that I have and possess . . .' (Exx 234).

We have seen in looking at Ignatius's images of the Trinity that God is present and active in the world in order to bring about the salvation of humanity; to rescue people from the self-destructive behaviour in which they can become trapped and to bring them to that fulness of life for which all are created. God does not impose this plan on us, however, as a totalitarian regime might impose on people what is considered to be good for them. On the contrary God invites people to collaborate in their own salvation and in promoting the salvation of others. God looks for partners not slaves, 'since the gentle arrangement of Divine Providence requires cooperation from his creatures' (*Constitutions*, 134). So Ignatius often uses his favourite image of himself and others as active, collaborative 'instruments in the hand of God' (*Constitutions*, 813, 814).

One of the criticisms often levelled against some forms of

Christian spirituality is that it throws people's attention too much on to eternity, the next life, and ignores the present world; that it promises future happiness at the expense of the real present and its pressing concerns. Ignatius's spirituality as a whole cannot justly be accused of this kind of other-worldliness, though we certainly feel its influence at some points of the *Spiritual Exercises*. His God, as we have seen, is very much present in this world, and invites people to collaborate in a project which takes place in this world. It has of course an other-worldly dimension: it would not be true to the gospel if it did not. The salvation which God promises and which people are invited to work for has its fulness in the next life. But it begins here, and Ignatius's image of the kingdom of God would not be genuinely Christian if it treated this present dimension as unimportant. The quality of our future salvation depends in large part on the quality of our involvement in building the kingdom of God on earth.

This leads to another aspect of Ignatius's image of God who is fully involved in all dimensions of human life. We have seen how in the Contemplation to Attain Love he stresses the presence of God in the histories of individual people. But God's presence and gifts are not confined to that. They extend through them to the institutions and structures by which both human life and the kingdom of God are sustained. When Ignatius agreed to found colleges, he was providing (in modern terms) 'graced' institutions through which the word and kingdom of God could be spread more widely. He also recognized that people in positions of responsibility and power influenced the structures of society, even to the extent of controlling them, and so were able to make those structures and institutions 'graced' or sinful means of promoting or hindering the kingdom of God.

Infinite goodness and wisdom

Christian faith and theology have attributed many qualities and powers to God in the course of time. Among them, judging by the number of times he refers to them, the qualities that seem to have meant most for Ignatius are God's goodness and wisdom. In all his writings he often refers to God by such titles as 'Infinite Goodness', 'Supreme Wisdom' and so on. The goodness of God, for him, is another term for God's love and the gifts that come from God. It describes the image of God that we have just been looking at: God who is so committed to the world in love as to be continuously giving to and working for humanity. But God's goodness and wisdom work together, for God's love is an ordered, effective love and God, 'as most perfect and infinite wisdom, is the beginning of all order' (*Constitutions*, 136). Together God's wisdom and goodness are very close to Dante's image of 'the love that moves the sun and the other stars'. So in the Preamble to the *Constitutions* Ignatius writes about the foundation of the Society: 'it must be the Supreme Wisdom and Goodness of God our Creator and Lord which will preserve, direct and carry forward in his divine service this least Society of Jesus, just as he deigned to begin it' (134). He saw the foundation of the Society, just as he saw his other projects, as a gift of God's goodness, and it was the supreme wisdom of God that enabled the project to be effectively carried through. Wisdom is also the gift that helps discernment, aids people to set order into life by choosing the right goals and the proper means to attain those goals. Human actions are rightly ordered when they are carried out under the influence of divine wisdom and attempt to embody this wisdom in human laws, structures and institutions. Once again it is worth noticing that, characteristically, Ignatius latches on to and emphasizes the practical effects of these attributes of God. As in all his images of God the verbs which describe what God does in and for the world, and in partnership with men and women, are far more important to him than adjectives which purport to describe aspects of God's own being 'in himself'.

I have stressed that Ignatius's images of God depict God as being very closely involved in the world, human history and the lives of individual people. On the other hand, however, we should not lose sight of the fact that for Ignatius God was by no means merely an immanent God. Though God is certainly active in the world, God is not part of created reality in the way that the rest of us are. God is apart, different. Some of the titles and images that Ignatius applies to God stress the transcendence of God. While it is true that he was used to knowing kings and lords as friends and companions in arms, nevertheless he also lived in an age which accepted absolute monarchy and the divine right of kings without much question. The king was seen as different from and above the rest of humanity. The picture of God as the Divine Majesty therefore brought home to him both the transcendence of God as the supreme lord of the whole of creation and the goodness of God in becoming one of us and becoming involved fully in our affairs. Sometimes too Ignatius explicitly stresses the differences between God and ourselves: 'I will consider who God is against whom I have sinned, going through his attributes and comparing them with their contraries in me: his wisdom with my ignorance, his power with my weakness, his justice with my iniquity, his goodness with my wickedness' (Exx 59; cf. Exx 237). God is mixed up in the world in very real and tangible ways, but in a sense that is possible only because God is also different, other, transcendent. And Ignatius has no difficulty keeping both of these two apparently contradictory features of God constantly in view.

Conclusions

In practical terms, of the images that we have looked at in this chapter those of Jesus and the Trinity are by far the most significant for Ignatius. It was Jesus who led him to the Trinity, and his contemplation of the work of the Trinity in the world led him back to focus on Jesus and to offer himself as a companion of Jesus in the service of people

In recent times Christian theology has taken a critical look at traditional formulations of belief and questioned some aspects of the mystery of the incarnation and Trinity as the traditions have presented them. At the same time our approaches to understanding the person and work of Jesus and our ways of reading scripture differ very considerably from those of Ignatius's time. It is important therefore that we do not allow ourselves to be caught in an uncritical literalistic approach to Ignatius's text and images. Entering into Ignatian spirituality today does not mean forcing ourselves to adopt as our own the images of Jesus and the Trinity which meant much to a sixteenth-century Basque and his contemporaries. There is little point in that, if it means the chafing bonds of literalism or the mental gymnastics of trying to force ourselves to live in an artificial time-warp.

Ignatius used the images of Jesus and the Trinity which appealed to him. Many of us come to Ignatian spirituality with images of Jesus and God already formed, and no doubt partly distorted. If Ignatius's own images are helpful to us, then of course we use them. In the Exercises especially we use Ignatius's suggestions as the starting-point and basis of our own contemplation and prayer. But it is also very important to grasp that Ignatius's spirituality also offers us the freedom to find, create if necessary, and develop the images of Jesus and the Trinity which speak to and answer the needs of our own experience and our own times, and to allow those images to come to expression. For that to happen we have to return constantly, as Ignatius did, to the sources of our images in scripture and the traditions of those Christians who have known, loved and served God well and who have left us images that we can contemplate. This allows our own images of Jesus to be challenged, confirmed and if necessary corrected by others'. It also helps us to marry, as Ignatius did for himself, images of Jesus and the Trinity in scripture and the traditions on the one hand and our own experience on the other, to help us to sustain a living relationship with God.

1　The sections I am referring to occur in pt I of the diary, 2 February to 12 March 1544: cf. *Spiritual Diary*, pp. 25–49. Ignatius's prose in the *Exercises* is laconic; in his diary it is spontaneous and often cryptic and is eventually reduced to a code.

2　*Letters*, pp. 125–6; cf. also *Constitutions*, 250.

3　*Letters*, p. 425.

4　*Spiritual Diary*, ss. 4, 13.

5　ibid. ss. 14, 15.

6　ibid. s. 34.

7   Michel de Certeau uses that phrase of Pierre Favre in his introduction to Favre's *Memorial*.
8   Gerard Manley Hopkins, 'The Wreck of the Deutschland', stanza 9.
9   *Letters*, pp. 318–19.
10 ibid. p. 321.
11 ibid. p. 336; cf. also pp. 347–9, 350–2, 355–6, 405–6.
12 ibid. p. 332.
13 *Spiritual Diary*, s. 15, p. 27.
14 ibid. s. 36, p. 31.
15 ibid. s. 15, p. 27.
16 ibid. s. 14, p. 27.

4

DISCERNMENT OF SPIRITS

It is not always recognized that discernment lies at the heart of Christian spirituality. People are even suspicious about the word 'discernment'. Some think that it is something so esoteric and technical as to be outside the scope of the ordinary Christian woman or man; others see it as another name for ordinary common sense enlightened by faith, and therefore not worth making a fuss about. In some religious circles too discernment jargon has become so over-used that it is all but meaningless. We often readily recognize, however, that if we take being a Christian fairly seriously, it involves us in daily attempts to make truth and love concrete realities. And discernment in the true sense of the word is essential to that enterprise.

Today we are more ready than we have been in the past to acknowledge that being a Christian is more of a search for genuine truth and love than a secure position of certainty from which to survey the world and pass judgement. Trying to be a Christian means learning how to respond with love to God, to people and to circumstances. It means searching for ways of living out the two great gospel commandments of loving God and our neighbour, while recognizing the imperfection of our attempts. It also means searching honestly for the most authentic truth; not just the knowledge that can be learned but makes little difference to how we live, but also the deeper gospel truth that makes little sense in fact until it becomes the truth which governs our lives.

The Christian's search for the way of truth and love however has another dimension which should not be forgotten, namely that it takes place within the setting of a living relationship with God 'who has loved us first', and who is seen as the source and revealer of the Christian way of truth and love. All genuine love implies a surrender. When I love another person I surrender all or part of myself to him or her; I allow part at least of my life to be, as it were, invaded and taken over by the other person. People say such things as: 'My life is not the same since I met her', or 'How Emma has changed since she met Frank'. When I love I allow another person to exercise a control and influence on me and my life which often astonishes both my friends and me by the radical changes it makes in the way I behave. And I make this surrender willingly and freely; it is not forced upon me. When the love is mutual the surrender, the offering of oneself to another, is mutual and there is both giving and receiving.

If our relationship with God is a relationship of love this too involves some form of surrender. If the relationship deepens we relinquish control of our own lives and hand this over to God, usually little by little, to the extent that we are able. This is not to say that we immaturely hand over responsibility for ourselves and our actions to another, but that we choose to collaborate with God. We allow God increasingly to lead us, though normally not without a struggle. This is the setting which discernment presupposes: a willingness to look at and appreciate the signs of God's love for us and in response to listen to the voice of the Spirit of God and to follow where the Spirit leads.

Our search draws us then to look for ways of making truth and love real in the shapes that our lives take, in all the changing circumstances in which we find ourselves. Because circumstances constantly change and the gospel is a living gospel and not a dead letter, Christian love and truth have constantly to be embodied and expressed in different forms. There is continuity with the past of course, but continuity does not mean simply repeating over and over again what has been done before. We have to find our own new ways of being Christians, of trying to live according to the gospel of Jesus, and discernment, rightly understood, is at the heart of this search for an authentic Christian discipleship.

Very briefly discernment is the art of appreciating the gifts that God has given us and discovering how we might best respond to that love in daily life. It is a process of finding one's own way of

discipleship in a particular set of circumstances; a means of responding to the call of Christian love and truth in a situation where there
are often conflicting interests and values and choices have to be
made. It is the gift by which we are able to observe and assess the
different factors in a particular situation, and to choose that course
of action which most authentically answers our desire to live by the
gospel.

Discernment of spirits is often associated with 'finding the will of
God', and there are difficulties about how we understand this.
Sometimes people talk about the will of God or the plan of God as
if it were a large, immensely complex, ever-changing, living blueprint of what God 'wants' to happen in the world. According to
this model, finding the will of God means something like getting in
touch with that small corner of the immense celestial blueprint that
concerns us, and getting to know 'what God wants us to do', so
that we can comply and thus 'do the will of God'. Of course that
short description is a caricature to some extent, but it contains
enough truth about the model that many people seem to use in
thinking and talking about 'the will of God'. And unfortunately it
is a powerful cause of anxiety to many good Christians who spend
much time and effort trying to 'find out' God's will according to
this model, and who became very distressed and anxious when, not
surprisingly, they do not succeed. There are many reasons why this
'management blueprint' model is unsatisfactory, but the principal
one I would like to mention here is the fact that it constricts our
freedom so much. The scope of our freedom is reduced to choosing
to fit in, whether we like it or not, with what God has 'planned' for
us, once we think we know what that is. And that is very little
freedom indeed.

A more satisfactory understanding of the will of God in connection with discernment of spirits gives greater value to our precious
gift of freedom. God's will for us is that we should learn to respond
in freedom to God's love for us, and to give shape to our individual
and common lives in freedom by the choices that we make. In
scripture, tradition, the Church, our own consciences and powers
of judgement and in many other gifts, God has given us aids to the
responsible exercise of our freedom. God's will is that we should

65

exercise our freedom responsibly and well by choosing what honestly seems the best course of action in a given set of circumstances, using all the relevant aids that we have been given for that purpose. There is a sense in which we create, in terms of concrete action in given circumstances, the will of God in this exercise of freedom. There is no blueprint in God's mind with which we have to comply. Discernment of spirits, within a living relationship with God, is one of the gifts that we have been given to help us to exercise our freedom in the choices that we make and so come to 'find the will of God' for us.

Discernment in Ignatius's life

It will help us to grasp the relevance of Ignatian discernment for ourselves if we look briefly at the part it played in the life of Ignatius himself. We have already seen that his conversion at Loyola awakened in him a deep attraction towards the person of Jesus, as he met him in Ludolph of Saxony's *Life of Christ*. And if we look at the life of Ignatius it is clear that there were two different but related settings in which discernment was at the heart of his following of Jesus. The one is the setting of everyday life; the other is those occasions on which he had a very important decision to make.

During and after his convalescence at Loyola he was moved by love for God and for Jesus to the extent that he began to want to give himself over to the service of God. His recognition that this would mean surrendering control of his life to God seems to have dawned gradually. The desire 'to find the will of God and to have the courage to carry it out' grew both more exciting and more insistent. He wanted to allow his life to be governed, not by his own desires and ambitions but by God, leading him in love, but it was some time before he learned exactly how he could put this into effect. He had to acquire a way of translating these powerful, even exhilarating desires into practical decisions which would shape his life for the future. And that meant two things: learning – from 'scratch', for he had no spiritual training to speak of – to grow in day-by-day responsiveness to God; and also to allow his major decisions about the direction of his life to be governed by the same openness to God's leading. In a word he had to learn discernment.

It was not from books nor from consulting people wise in the ways of the spirit that Ignatius took the first steps in discernment, but by noting and reflecting on his own experience. During his convalescence he began to observe that different possible options open to him for the future evoked different responses in him. Thoughts of continuing to live as he had lived before, or daydreams in which he idealized himself as a romantic hero, though pleasant while they lasted, ultimately left him feeling sad and dissatisfied. On the other hand when he pictured in his mind the wonderful things he might do for God – even difficult and painful things like walking barefoot to Jerusalem and eating nothing but herbs – he experienced deep feelings of joy which left him satisfied and cheerful. From noting and reflecting on these two sets of feelings, and on the direction in which they seemed to be leading him, he concluded that the way God wanted him to follow was becoming clear to him. God was speaking to him through his experience. He would go as a pilgrim to Jerusalem (Autobiography, 8).

There is not space here to give a stage-by-stage account of Ignatius's education in discernment.[1] Naturally some of his experiences – including the most painful ones – contributed more than others to his education. At Manresa he had to learn how to deal with (among other things) the onset of a real distaste for anything which had to do with God; persistent waves of discouragement about the way of life he was taking up; serious illnesses which brought him again to the point of death; scruples so bad that they nearly drove him to suicide, and 'consolations' so powerful that they made his eyes hurt with weeping (Autobiography, 19–34). Then and later he also grew in the art of knowing how to distinguish between true and false forms of encouragement, enthusiasm and other pleasant and satisfying feelings. In Jerusalem he discovered that, though he had been right to go there, it was impossible for him to stay as he had intended and he must find God's purpose for him over again. He was brought before the Inquisition for trial and put in prison more than once. Between Salamanca and Paris he was discouraged because his original group of companions broke up and dispersed.

In Barcelona and Paris he enjoyed powerful spiritual insights which absorbed his attention and threatened to wreck his studies and deflect him from his purpose. Later on in Rome his concept of the Society of Jesus was threatened when the authorities objected to its lack of monastic or conventual structures and practices and actually imposed Office in choir for a time.[2]

That is by no means the whole story but it is enough to see the kind of experiences Ignatius used to learn and practise discernment. Through these and other storms, as well as in smoother seas, he tried to find his own personal way and to be faithful to that. From the time of his stay at Manresa onwards, of course, he had opportunities to consult people skilled in discernment of spirits, and eventually he had access to books which could teach him the tradition and principles of discernment, particularly during his studies. But he began with his own experience, and his later reading added to, confirmed and no doubt modified what he had learned there.

After his return from Jerusalem in 1523 his main intention was to devote himself to 'helping souls'. His writings on discernment, brief though they are, form one of his most valuable and original legacies for others who are engaged in pastoral work, and particularly in spiritual direction. Occasionally Ignatius himself wrote letters of direction in which he explained some of the principles of discernment.[3] But the *Spiritual Exercises* are the book in which he formally set out his guidelines for others to use. There the two sets of Rules for the Discernment of Spirits define some of the technical terms, explain the fundamental principles of discernment, and offer acute and sensitive guidance in dealing with typical situations that arise, especially when evil masquerades as good or the less good as the better. Here and there in the sections known as the Annotations and the Additional Directions, Ignatius also offers a few further helps towards discernment. And the sections of the *Exercises* that deal with an Election, taken in conjunction with these rules, provide the spiritual guide with a step-by-step approach to discernment, in the particular context of helping a person make an important decision. Taken together these are an original and extraordinarily thorough guide to discernment and Christian decision-making. They speak specifically to the context of giving and making the

Exercises, but by no means exclusively, and they have been found to have much wider and very helpful application in daily life.[4]

Ignatian discernment of spirits: principles and practice

Discernment of spirits in everyday life involves us in a process of sifting our daily experience by noting and reflecting regularly on our affective responses to God and to life and its events. It means noting, for example, situations and events in which we experience joy or sorrow, peace or turmoil, attractions or revulsions, an opening out to others or a narrowing in on ourselves, a sense of God's presence or absence, creativity or destructiveness. The purpose of observing and reflecting on these patterns of responses is that they deepen our sense of ourselves and they can show us where, for each of us, our Christian path lies, where the Spirit of God is leading. Those are large claims and demand an explanation.

To help our explanation I will make two more preliminary remarks. The first is that discernment of spirits is concerned with choices between two options or values both of which appear to be morally good. The process aims at determining what is the right or better choice in particular given circumstances. Often it is a choice between two courses both of which initially appear morally good and then later, when the discernment process has matured, one of them looks different. This different colour may not be downright evil but might be such as to involve a spurning of love.

A second preliminary note has to do with the fact that the term 'discernment of spirits' harks back to a previous age of psychology. The term itself comes from the time when the variety and changes of often contrary feelings within the human person were attributed to the presence and action of 'good' spirits (the Spirit of God and the angels) and 'evil' spirits (Satan and his minions). Naturally Ignatius, being a man of his pre-Freudian time, accepted this framework unquestioningly and built it automatically into his writing on discernment. But of course we do not have to accept that particular theoretical framework in order to believe in and practise discernment. A difficulty is, however, that we have not yet found a very adequate terminology to replace the traditional one, and people still use the language of 'spirits'. So it is important to distinguish between this language and the outmoded theoretical framework from which it springs, and to know what we in fact mean if we use the language of 'spirits'.

With those observations in mind, we can now look more closely at the fundamentals of discernment in the Ignatian tradition. Though Ignatius and his companions also practised 'group discernment', our primary focus here is on the individual person rather than a group. Group discernment is largely an adaptation of the principles and process of individual discernment.

In the course of everyday life we experience a continuous, sometimes bewildering succession and mixture of different affective movements: desires, revulsions, attractions, impulses and feelings of varying intensity and power. We know too that we have different levels of feeling: some of our desires and responses are superficial; we recognize them and are affected by them but they do not engage us deeply as persons. I can be moved even to tears, for example, by watching a romantic film, but the feelings which it evokes are usually fairly transient emotions which do not affect in a notable way my conduct or my more lasting attitudes and commitments. Other states of feeling however are far deeper and more significant: the experience of falling in love, for instance, can be a profound affective movement which alters my conduct more or less radically, touches me at the level of my most cherished beliefs, attitudes, desires and commitments and changes me permanently. In between these two levels of feeling, of course, there are many others. In discernment of spirits it is the deeper levels of affectivity that we are concerned with: those which actually influence our behaviour; the areas where our affective life and the life of the spirit interpenetrate; the places from which spring our commitments, our most significant choices and the fundamental directions that we give to our lives. Discernment is mainly about those more significant areas of our affective life.

These movements or states of feeling that we experience can be evoked by events and people in the external world or by our own thoughts, imagination, dreams, our own 'inner world'. Sometimes too their origin seems to be largely physiological, as in some kinds of depression. Often enough we do not know where the feelings come from or why we feel as we do. In discernment of spirits it is not the origin of a particular affective state or movement that is the main issue, though to know that can be helpful. Discernment has to do more with the spiritual interpretation and evaluation of feelings, and particularly with the direction in which we are moved by them.

Ignatius identified two contrary kinds of feelings or affective movements among those which we experience. They are contrary in that, when they affect us, they move us in opposite directions. In the tradition of discernment which Ignatius grew familiar with, they are called 'consolation' and 'desolation'. (Ignatius's own descriptions of consolation and desolation are in sections 316–17 of the *Spiritual Exercises*). Very briefly consolation is any affective movement or state that draws us to God or that helps us to be less centred upon ourselves and to open out to others in generosity, service and love. We might feel, for example, a sense of gratitude to God that leads us to a deeper faith, trust and love; or a joyful awareness and appreciation of the presence and action and gifts of God in people, in events in our own lives or in some other part of the world; we might experience a state of peace and quiet in the knowledge of God and God's gifts, and so reach out to others in reconciliation and trust. All these, and others, are examples of the kind of movements of feeling that the umbrella term 'consolation' includes. The main feature of them is that their direction is towards growth, creativity and a genuine fulness of life and love in that they draw us to a fuller, effective, generous love of God and other people, and to a right love of ourselves.

The feelings and affective movements that come under the heading of 'desolation' are the contrary of these. Their characteristic tendency is to draw us away from God and things which have to do with God, and to lead us to be self-centred, closed in and unconcerned about God or other people. These feelings move us in the opposite direction from the previous ones. So, for example, we might feel a depressing inner darkness and restlessness; life ceases to have meaning; God and other people seem to count for nothing;

paralysing feelings of failure, guilt and self-hatred can threaten to set us on a downward spiral of neglect of ourselves, other people and God; or we might experience other states and movements of feeling which seem to undermine our capacities for faith, hope and love and to lead us into destructive forms of behaviour towards others and ourselves.[5]

The crucial issue therefore in interpreting and evaluating our feelings in discernment is not so much where the movement of feeling is coming from (though knowledge of this can of course be helpful) nor even what exactly the feeling is: joy, anger, guilt, confusion and so on. It is rather the direction in which the feelings are leading. But it is also very important to realize that in discernment our interpretation and estimate of the spiritual value of any affective movement depends upon the context in which it occurs. Let us take an example. Peter is a man who takes his Christian life fairly seriously, wants to deepen as far as he can his relationship with God and to live out the consequences of his discipleship in his attitudes towards other people and the world and in his dealings with them. That is the general direction of his life, and normally he will find joy and peace in events and people and choices which are consistent with these desires. If he experiences movements of feeling that we usually associate with desolation, it could be an indication in him of a resistance to this direction; some inner movement that is contrary to this general direction and thus causing him to experience conflict within himself; something that is threatening to deflect him from his commitment.

Mark on the other hand is a man who has little time for God and little consideration for other people. On his own admission he is mainly interested in 'looking after number one' as much as he can, and is not averse to exploitation and manipulation of other people, with an eye to the main chance. If he finds himself experiencing feelings we usually associate with desolation – restlessness, confusion, sadness and depression, for instance – it can be a sign that there is a movement within him that is contrary to this general direction of his life and wants him to change it. The human spirit seeks goodness and truth rather than the opposite and tries to reassert those values in people who neglect them.

72

The main point about the two examples is that the same feelings – in this case restlessness, confusion, disturbance, lack of peace – have opposite significance for discernment. In the case of Peter they indicate a destructive movement to draw him away from living out faithfully his Christian commitment; whereas for Mark the same kind of feelings show the presence of a movement towards growth through taking more notice of the kinds of values we associate with Christianity.

The decisive difference lies in the general direction in which the two men's lives are moving. In the old terminology: Peter interprets these feelings as evidence of the 'evil spirit' trying to lead him towards what is less good; in Mark's case they are signs of a 'good spirit' trying to move him to a better way. Most commonly in discernment we are dealing with a person like Peter, one who wants to grow in Christian discipleship. In this case 'consolation' will mean pleasant feelings of joy, peace, delight in God and in the following of Jesus, and 'desolation' will mean unpleasant feelings: confusion, sadness, moods of depression, distaste for the things involved in the following of Jesus.

There is another important point to make about desolation. It is natural to judge any kind of desolation as bad, because the experience is usually painful and for a committed Christian the direction in which it is leading is destructive. Ignatius is at pains to insist, however, that desolation, far from being necessarily harmful and bad, can in fact be an experience of growth if it is handled well (Exx 318–22). The feelings of desolation, whatever form they may take, are not in themselves destructive. But if we begin to act and to make choices under the influence of feelings of desolation, that is when it becomes destructive for ourselves and for others. Ignatius's advice therefore is that we should not make any changes or any decisions in time of and under the influence of feelings of desolation, precisely because they could be destructive and lead us away from God.

The process of discernment of spirits therefore is one of looking at and sifting our present and past experience, taking note especially of the events, people and situations that are associated with or evoke the moods and feelings of consolation and desolation. When we look at the present and immediate future in this way the aim of discernment is to help us to make choices which encourage and build on the events and situations that are associated with consolation. The reason behind this is that it is characteristic of the Spirit of God to produce consolation, to work for that which is life-giving, creative, joyful, peaceful and so on – the fruits of the Spirit. So our past experiences of consolation show us times when the Spirit has been at work in our lives. And in the present and future our path of truth and growth in discipleship is to choose those ways of being, those courses of action that bring consolation, for that is to respond to the Spirit's leading.

Let us look at another example. Pauline was a teacher for ten years and then took a job in administration in industry. The salary was higher, she had less distance to travel to work each day and the administrative post matched her qualifications. Five years later, in the course of a retreat, she begins to reflect on her present and past experience because she feels dissatisfied, unhappy, restless and out of place in her work. Her reflection on her experiences of 'consolation' and 'desolation' brings home to her that her feelings of consolation are in fact associated with teaching, and her opposite feelings are associated with her present work, although there seemed to be excellent reasons for changing jobs when she did. For her teaching was creative, life-giving, a source of joy and peace, while her present job now appears to be destructive. Her way forward might be to look at possible job options which could allow her to find work which was once again a source of consolation. On the other hand once she has realised what has been happening she might also be able to approach her present job in such a way that she begins to find consolation where previously she found the opposite.

There are other depths and vagaries of the human heart that Ignatius lays bare, especially in his second set of guidelines for discernment (Exx 329–36). In particular he highlights the fact that feelings of consolation can be deceptive: 'the devil hath power to assume a pleasing shape'.[6] Feelings of consolation – joy, peace, encouragement, enthusiasm, delight – can in fact lead to a result which is less good and even destructive.

This fact, that there is false as well as true consolation, is obviously very important to remember in discernment. And Ignatius records an experience of it in his own life which helps to clarify it for us. During the time of his studies, both in Barcelona and again in Paris, the insights that he had into spiritual matters were one of his sources of great delight (Autobiography, 55, 82). He found he could spend a long time thinking about these things with great joy, peace and satisfaction: they were a source of consolation to him and good things in themselves. The disadvantage however was that they distracted him from his studies to the extent that he could not concentrate on the lectures. (Perhaps what he felt was the effect of an unconscious resistance within himself to the prospect of going back to secondary school at his age and in real poverty. In the circumstances his desire to escape into his 'spiritual thoughts' is understandable!) Eventually he came to the conclusion that they were what he called a deceptive form of consolation. Though good in themselves they were in fact drawing him away from his better purpose, which was to study in order to be able to help other people. The wise and successful step that he took to be free of the deception was to tell one of his teachers what was happening to him, and to promise 'never to fail to attend your class these two years, as long as I can find bread and water for my support' (Autobiography, 55).

The advice that Ignatius offers for such instances in his guidelines is no doubt based on this and similar experiences. Deceptive consolation is subtle. We often only recognise that it is deceptive and harmful after some time when its true, destructive effect becomes clear, by its 'serpent's tail', as Ignatius says (Exx 334). By then, of course, harm may have been done. The response that Ignatius advises is twofold. First we should trace back from the harmful effect the whole chain of thoughts and feelings to the point where things started to go wrong (Exx 333–4). This will also help us to notice the deception more easily in the future. And the second piece of advice is to tell somebody about what is happening. This enables someone who is outside the situation to look at it more objectively and not to be taken in so easily by the deception. Or, as Ignatius puts it with much more colour and drama:

Our enemy may also be compared in his manner of acting to a false lover. He seeks to remain hidden and does not want to be discovered. If such a lover speaks with evil intention to the daughter of a good father, or to the wife of a good husband, and seeks to seduce them, he wants his words and solicitations kept secret . . . In the same way when the enemy of our human nature tempts a just soul with his wiles and seductions, he earnestly desires that they be received secretly and kept secret. But if one manifests them to a confessor, or to some other spiritual person who understands his deceits and malicious designs, the evil one is very much vexed. For he knows that he cannot succeed in his evil undertaking, once his evident deceits have been revealed (Exx 326).

Discernment and choices: the Election

Ignatius recognizes the fact that a person who is making the Spiritual Exercises might come to the point of making a fundamental decision about her or his own life in the course of the Exercises. So in the material for the Second Week he offers a series of aids for making what has come to be called the Election (i.e. the Choice or Decision). These aids, taken together, make up a process of Christian decision-making based on discernment of spirits. And although these aids are set in the particular context of the Exercises, the principles and methods they embody are also very helpful when adapted for decision-making in everyday life. I am going to discuss Ignatius's guidelines in some detail here because I believe that the help that he offers towards making good decisions is one of his more distinctive and valuable contributions to Christian living, with undoubted application to our circumstances today.

The context of the Exercises is a particularly helpful one for making an important decision. The person who is making the Exercises is living in an atmosphere of prayer and reflection in which he or she is able to be more open than is usual in everyday life to God and to the various inner movements which we have been discussing in this chapter. These movements and their significance have been the subject of daily conversations between the one who is making the Exercises and her or his 'director'. During the First Week those who are making the Exercises have become more aware of the interior and exterior bonds which impede them in their responses to God's love and faithfulness, and in their attempts to follow Christ in freedom. We can hope too that in the process they have also become at least a little more free from the destructive effects of those bonds, though this kind of liberation also continues long after they have finished making the Exercises.

At the beginning of the Second Week they have looked in some detail at the fundamental demands and framework of discipleship of Jesus when contemplating at length and repeatedly (Exx 118–31) the Call of the King (Exx 91–8), the story of the incarnation (Exx 101–9), the nativity of Jesus (Exx 110–17) and aspects of his early life (Exx 132–4). They are therefore coming to the point of looking again at the life and teaching of Jesus in the gospels, the world in which they live and their own lives and noticing resonances and discords, harmonies and disharmonies between them. In the contemplation on the Call of the King and in subsequent periods of prayer over several days they have been invited to offer themselves generously to follow and serve Jesus (Exx 98), and they have prayed repeatedly for 'an intimate knowledge of Our Lord . . . that I may love him more and follow him more closely' (Exx 104). In the Meditation on Two Standards and at other times they have contemplated personal and social dimensions of the setting in which their lives are placed in the light of the gospels and the mission of Jesus. They may therefore be in a position to examine and choose (or renew a choice already made of) the way in which they hope to put into effect their commitment to Jesus in the particular circumstances of their own lives. And that, in some form, is usually the basic material of the Election.

As the decision is about how a person is going to follow Jesus in his or her own life, the process of discernment in the time of decision-making, as indeed throughout the Exercises, goes on within the framework of that person's understanding of himself or herself in relation to the larger world together with daily contemplation of gospel events from the life of Jesus. The inner, affective movements of consolation and desolation, therefore, are responses to the gospel accounts of Jesus's life, death and resurrection, to the exercitant's own life and to the world generally. Jesus's way is kept firmly in view all the time, however, and the decision is made in very close relation to that. To help discernment still further Ignatius sets out the Contemplation on Two Standards (Exx 136–48). There he asks one who makes the Exercises to look at again and try to understand more fully discipleship of Jesus, and especially the contrary objectives and ways of operating of Jesus and 'the enemy of our human nature': the one life-giving, the other destructive.

Throughout his guidelines for the Election, Ignatius is concerned that circumstances should be right for making a decision (Exx 170), and that the person faced with the choice should be motivated as far as possible by a single intention: 'the service and praise of God our Lord and the salvation of my soul' (Exx 169). So he offers for repeated consideration a series of examples, some of them short parables, which illustrate bad, good and better choices (Exx 149–56, 165–8), culminating in this statement of the worthiest grounds for choosing:

> Whenever the praise and glory of the Divine Majesty would be equally served, in order to imitate and be in reality more like Christ our Lord, I desire and choose poverty with Christ poor, rather than riches; insults with Christ loaded with them rather than honours; I desire to be accounted as worthless and a fool for Christ, rather than to be esteemed as wise and prudent in this world. So Christ was treated before me. (Exx 167)

The Election

Ignatius's step-by step guidance for the Election is discernment in slow motion. We should remember, of course, that throughout the Election the one who is making the Exercises is discussing his or her inner affective movements daily with the person who gives the Exercises. Ignatius envisaged three different situations in which a person might come to a decision:

1 He takes into account, first the possibility that the Spirit of God simply moves a person to make the right choice 'so that a devout soul without hesitation or the possibility of hesitation, follows what has been manifested to it' (Exx 175). His own examples of this are Matthew the tax-gatherer in the gospels and Saul on the Damascus road.

2 The second situation, which is obviously more usual, happens when a person experiences different affective and spiritual movements of consolation and desolation such as we have been discussing. Discernment here means observing and reflecting on the pattern of those experiences and making the choice which is associated with feelings of consolation (cf. Exx 176).

3 It can happen of course that the person who is making the decision experiences, not the see-saw of two contrary kinds of feeling but 'a time of tranquillity, that is, a time when the soul is not agitated by different spirits, and has free and peaceful use of its natural powers' (Exx 177). This third situation is the time when it is appropriate and even necessary to use some different methods of approaching the decision.

3.1 The first of these is a systematic consideration, not this time of the *feelings* that are evoked by the decision, but of all the *reasons* for and against the various options; the advantages and disadvantages of each possible choice (cf. Exx 178–183).

3.2 In the second of these methods for 'a time of tranquillity' Ignatius suggests some exercises by which those who are making the Election, by use of the imagination, can place themselves in circumstances where they would want to make the right choice (Exx 184–8). Having done that they should consider what decision would be right, and allow themselves to be guided by that.

The wise purpose behind Ignatius's guidelines for a decision in 'a time of tranquillity' is that he is trying to ensure that three necessary elements are present. The first of these is that the person who is making the decision not only reflects on how he or she *feels* about it but also weighs carefully all the circumstances and factors that are relevant to the decision, and especially all possible reasons both for and against each of the options. This helps to avert the danger of making a wrong choice under the influence of powerful feeling such as enthusiasm or depression, without attempting a realistic appraisal of the situation. His second purpose is to try to ensure as much objectivity as possible on the part of the person making the choice (Exx 185–7 especially). And thirdly he tries to make sure that this person knows as well as possible his or her motives and objectives in the decision. To help to achieve this he repeatedly points out what he sees as the most worthy grounds on which good choices can be made (Exx 177, 179, 180, 181, 183, 184, 185, 189).

Offering and confirmation

In the Exercises the Election takes place in an atmosphere of prayer, as is fitting for any important decision which a Christian person makes. Prayer is part of the process of decision-making in a distinctive way. We have seen how the decision is made during a time of repeated contemplation of the life and teaching of Jesus as presented in the gospels, so that Jesus is a constant reference-point. Moreover the person who makes the decision looks at all the advantages and disadvantages of his or her options in a time of prayerful tranquillity, and is constantly begging God for help and guidance. And the exercises which Ignatius proposes as part of the Election itself are prayer exercises.

Prayer also becomes an essential part of the Election in one other very important way. Ignatius advises that when the choice has been made, we should repeatedly offer our choice to God 'that the Divine Majesty may deign to accept and confirm it, if it is for his greater service and praise' (Exx 183; cf. Exx 188). The offering is a sign of the desire to choose what we believe will most give praise and service to God.

Once the decision has been made Ignatius expects that we will experience confirmation of the rightness of our choice, and that this confirmation will come through experiences of consolation. This will assure us that the decision we have reached is coherent with and a concrete expression of our commitment to being disciples of Jesus.

In the context of the Exercises the Third and Fourth Weeks are very important as the setting in which the decision is confirmed. Contemplation of the passion and death of Jesus in particular can be a time when our commitment to Jesus and our faithfulness to the decision we have made are severely challenged by the cross, as we contemplate more fully the implications of our choice. Consolation at that time can be a very encouraging confirmation. Outside the Exercises confirmation of our right choices comes with time: sometimes in prayer; equally also in the continuing experience of consolation in daily life, as we try to live out our choices and commitments in circumstances which are never ideal. A wrong choice will be expected to lead in these same circumstances to experiences of desolation. For these reasons it is very important that discernment continues after an important decision has been made.

Reflections

It should now be easier to see why discernment is at the heart of Ignatian spirituality, and to understand the claim that it also lies at the heart of any genuine Christian spirituality. We have been used to thinking that spirituality has mainly to do with the 'inner life', prayer, mysticism and so on. But these things form only a part of it, though a not unimportant part. They are incomplete except within a broader setting in which disciples of Jesus try to live their discipleship in committed, honest and coherent ways. And discernment is at the heart of discipleship, because when we walk a disciple's path we are constantly faced with changing situations in which we have to discover how to be faithful to the gospel and the leading of the Spirit, and true to ourselves.

This involves us constantly in making choices, in our attempts to integrate prayer and life. Some of them are the great decisions involved in our fundamental commitments or when we make significant changes of direction. But there are also the lesser, daily choices by which, within the larger context of our basic commitments, we give shape to our everyday lives. We have seen in this chapter what Ignatius has to offer to us in both the larger and the smaller choices.

Finally, because of common misapprehensions, it is important to remind ourselves that Christian discernment and decision-making are not automatic or mechanical processes. The guidelines offered by Ignatius are not like the instruction manual for using the word-processor on which I have written this chapter. With the manual, so long as the instructions are correct and I follow them accurately and the machine is functioning properly, the word processor will store and eventually print the chapter. Ignatius's guidelines are not a manual for operating a machine nor are they a magic spell for infallibly producing a right answer. It is not true to say that if I follow to the letter the instructions about decision-making set out in the Exercises I will automatically come out with the guaranteed 'right' decision. Decision-making on a particular occasion by discernment of spirits presupposes a living relationship with God and a background of daily life in which I am trying to be responsive and faithful to the Spirit's leading. That is the only context in which Ignatius's guidelines have meaning and use. And a 'right' decision about a course of action I should take is not a matter of finding out some so far undiscovered item of 'God's plan' and putting it into effect. Rather the 'right' decision is what appears to be the best in the circumstances and is the expression of the deepest truths of ourselves within the setting of this day-to-day relationship with God.

1   Nicholas King, 'Ignatius Loyola and decision-making' *The Way Supplement* 24 (Spring 1975), pp. 46–57, traces the growth of Ignatius's experience of discernment with regard to choices.
2   cf. e.g. Dalmases, op. cit. pp. 169–72, 285–7.
3   His most famous letter on discernment is that to Sister Teresa Rejadell in *Letters*, pp. 18–25; other letters which deal with some aspects of discernment can be seen in ibid. pp. 126–30, 179–82, 196–211, 257–8, 420–1.

4 A good book which in a helpful way translates Ignatius's guidance in discernment from the setting of the Exercises to that of daily life is John English, *Spiritual Freedom* (Loyola House, Guelph, Ontario, 1982).
5 Gerard W. Hughes has a useful chapter on interpreting and evaluating these feelings in *God of Surprises* (Darton, Longman and Todd, London, 1985). He writes of consolation and desolation in terms of 'creative moods' and 'destructive moods'.
6 William Shakespeare, *Hamlet*, Act 2, sc. ii.

5

IGNATIAN PRAYER

When people talk about 'Ignatian prayer' they usually mean the typical form of imaginative contemplation outlined in the *Spiritual Exercises*. But it is important to stress that the book of the Exercises contains a large number and variety of forms of prayer or 'spiritual exercises' that Ignatius himself had found helpful at different times, especially when he was learning to pray at Loyola during his convalescence and later at Manresa. The *Exercises*, however, are not a book about prayer in the modern sense. From one point of view, (though perhaps not the most important one), what Ignatius offers in the *Spiritual Exercises* can be seen as an ordered sequence of practical guidelines which can be used to introduce people to a wide range of different ways of praying, initially within the setting of an enclosed retreat but also of course appropriate to the varied circumstances of everyday life.

Contemplation

In this chapter I shall give particular attention to two typical kinds of Ignatian prayer: first what Ignatius calls 'contemplation' with its emphasis on using the imagination in a particular way and, later, the form of prayer and reflection that goes by the name of the 'examen'.[1]

In the history of Christian spirituality the words 'contemplation' and 'contemplative' have had a number of very different meanings. Often they have been used to denote the kind of prayer that is appropriate to people who are 'advanced' on the path of prayer, rather than to beginners. Ignatius however does not restrict his use of these words to designate the so-called 'higher' forms of prayer. By contemplation he means a particular approach to prayer which is open to beginners as well as to those more experienced in the life of prayer, though there are clearly differences in the approach to and experience of contemplation in accordance with the stage of one's growth in prayer.

In the authentic Ignatian tradition 'contemplation' means something fairly definite and distinctive. It is very sad that Ignatian prayer has often been wrongly depicted as a form of meditation that is on the one hand rigid and on the other hand abstract, intellectual and theological, with little or no connection with affectivity and the heart. Ignatius himself used both terms, 'meditation' and 'contemplation', but even 'meditation' in his vocabulary is not an intellectual, speculative exercise.[2] As we have seen he did not have a speculative mind; he was not at home with abstract thought and had little gift for it. His mind worked far more easily with the concrete, with stories, pictures and images. When he presents the Christian mysteries and truths in the *Exercises*, for example, he does so mainly by means of stories and pictures. He asks the one making the Exercises to recall 'the history', 'see the place', look at what the people in the story or picture are doing and listen to what they are saying. His presentation of the central mystery of the incarnation, for instance, which has often been the subject of highly abstract, speculative thought among theologians, takes the very effective form of a series of pictures, scenes which form a story (Exx 101–9; 110–17 etc.). It would be a mistake to think that the form of contemplation which Ignatius used was invented by him. One of his gifts was an ability to pick up from a tradition elements which he found helpful and to develop them for his own use. This is what he did with imaginative contemplation, which had already been widely practised in medieval monastic circles as well as being adapted for the circumstances of life of lay people.

Ignatius's outline of the contemplation of the nativity of Jesus in the *Exercises* will serve us as a typical example of an 'Ignatian contemplation' which takes as its subject-matter a story from the gospels (Exx 110–17).

The Second Contemplation
The Nativity

PRAYER. The usual preparatory prayer.

FIRST PRELUDE. This is the history of the mystery. Here it will be that Our Lady, about nine months with child, and, as may be piously believed, seated on an ass, set out from Nazareth. She was accompanied by Joseph and a maid, who was leading an ox. They are going to Bethlehem to pay the tribute that Caesar imposed on those lands.

SECOND PRELUDE. This is a mental representation of the place. It will consist here in seeing in imagination the way from Nazareth to Bethlehem. Consider its length, its breadth; whether level or through valleys and over hills. Observe also the place or cave where Christ is born; whether big or little; whether high or low; and how it is arranged.

THIRD PRELUDE. This will be the same as in the preceding contemplation and identical in form with it (i.e. This is to ask for what I desire. Here it will be to ask for an intimate knowledge of our Lord, who has become incarnate for me, that I may love him more and follow him more closely.)

FIRST POINT. This will consist in seeing the persons, namely, Our Lady, St Joseph, the maid, and the Child Jesus after his birth. I will make myself a poor little unworthy slave, and as though present, look upon them, contemplate them, and serve them in their needs with all possible homage and reverence.

Then I will reflect on myself, that I may reap some fruit.

SECOND POINT. This is to consider, observe and contemplate what the persons are saying, and then to reflect on myself and to draw some fruit from it.

THIRD POINT. This is will be to see and consider what they are doing, for example, making the journey and laboring that our Lord might be born in extreme poverty, and that after many labors, after hunger, thirst, heat and cold, after insults and out-rages, he might die on the cross and all this for me.

Then I will reflect and draw some spiritual fruit from what I have seen.

COLLOQUY. Close with a colloquy as in the preceding contemplation, and with the Our Father.

This outline of a contemplation, as given by Ignatius, is certainly very structured and may even seem rigid and constricting. Today many people reject 'Ignatian contemplation'. It was offered to them in the past and was like a strait-jacket, usually because of the way in which it was presented. The contemplation is structured here because Ignatius had an orderly mind, and in these meditations and contemplations in the *Exercises* he is engaged in introducing to prayer people who have good will, generosity and a desire to pray but often little idea how to go about it in practice. The structure is meant as a means of liberation, not as a strait-jacket; it is a step-by-step guide by the use of which each person can find his or her own personal way of praying. It is vitally important to remember, in learning to pray or in teaching others, that Ignatius's methods and structures are not ends in themselves or paths to be slavishly followed; they are intended to set people free to find the way of praying that suits them individually, and experience shows that, rightly used, they do this powerfully.

The subject-matter of Ignatian contemplation is typically some aspect of God's dealings with the world, especially as revealed in the images and stories of scripture. In Chapter 2 I described how Ignatius was powerfully attracted to Jesus, and in the Exercises the gospel stories of Jesus form much of the subject-matter for contemplation. Implicit in this form of prayer too there is a particular understanding of the function and importance of scripture, and of the gospels in particular. The gospels are the means by which God addresses each individual person in the circumstances of his or her own life. They are an important document which mediates God to each of us here and now. By means of this form of contemplation we are able to open our hearts and minds to hear the word of God as fully as possible, to allow it to sink into our consciousness and to influence our feelings and our most important commitments and choices. Consequently this form of prayer, centred on the word of God or on events which likewise mediate God to us, is a formative process. It can mould and change us in accordance with the word of God, and can reach our innermost hearts, the most fundamental attitudes and dispositions which day by day give shape and colour to our lives. This form of imaginative contemplation helps people to put on 'the mind of Christ'.

God is most clearly mediated to us through easily recognized religious images such as biblical writings and stories, accepted religious symbols and rituals and people whose lives obviously speak to us of God. But it is characteristic of Ignatian contemplation to extend the range of images in which God is to be found so as to recognize and contemplate God 'in all things'. This is based upon a particular understanding of created reality by which the whole created world is seen as an image which mediates the presence of God to us in various forms, and as the arena in which God is continuously at work.[3] If God is also really present and active in the world at every level of being, if the world truly is a sacrament of God, who is Lord of creation, and Lord of history, then any reality in the world, person, event or object can become an image of God and a focus of contemplation. So we find images of God in the beauty of the universe itself, in our own communal or personal history and experience, in events, in people's words and actions, in the structures and institutions that we create, in great human achievements and even in suffering, poverty and hardship.

It is important to note however that this does not imply the naive and unrealistic view that all events and all people's actions and words are immediately and transparently a divine epiphany. The world is shot through with ambiguity and forces in opposition. Ignatius expresses this in his own way in the Meditation on Two Standards in the *Exercises* (136–48), where he depicts the world, our relationships, institutions, social structures and each person as a scene of a great conflict between the forces of Christ on the one hand and 'the enemy of our human nature' on the other, a conflict from which no person and no aspect of life is excluded. Our words and actions, our lives as a whole and the structures and institutions that we create can embody the grace of God; they can also embody the opposite, sin and darkness rather than light and grace. Ignatian contemplation involves learning to discriminate in this mixture and to contemplate the presence and action of God within that ambiguity and conflict (Exx 139).

Ignatian contemplation is a form of prayer that engages the whole person and all one's powers. Contrary to what has often been taught, it is not purely 'mental prayer' or a form of discursive meditation on abstract truths, but rather an activity or movement of the whole person, and especially of the heart, towards God. That is why Ignatius insists, for example, that the prayer environment, bodily posture and health, the amount and kinds of food that a person takes and other apparently mundane features all affect one's capacity to pray.[4] As we have seen in the contemplation on the nativity, if the stories or events which form the subject-matter for prayer are not actually physically present to us, memory recalls them. Imagination makes them vivid to us and allows us to work with them creatively, by helping us to be present, for example, to a gospel scene, and in imagination to hold a conversation with people in the story (Exx 109 etc.). We explore the stories and images with the mind, respond to them with our feelings, interact with them in imagination, reflect on them in solitude and calm and allow these varied activities ultimately to influence our choices and commitments (Exx 1–2, 111–17 etc.). The senses too are not to be left out, for the process of contemplation can also mean bringing all our senses to bear on images, events and stories which mediate God to us, either when they are physically and immediately present to us or by a process of 'applying the senses' to images held in the memory and imagination (Exx 66–71, 121–6).

While this kind of contemplation engages the whole person with the varied capacities and powers that belong to the human person, it also gives a special place to imagination and the different levels of feeling and commitment which can be touched and moved through the imagination. Ignatius is particularly concerned that through the imagination a person should be drawn to God in love (Exx 3). And so he recommends that the 'contemplation' should include what he calls a colloquy – a conversation in which the person praying expresses freely and with confidence the feelings that have been aroused by the contemplation, 'as one friend speaks to another' (Exx 54). Imaginative contemplation of the gospels moves the heart and in the 'colloquy' the heart speaks out of its fulness or emptiness.

Ignatius recognized of course that developments take place in people's style of contemplation. In the Exercises he expects, for example, that prayer will simplify and that those who make the Exercises will need progressively less material. The method that he calls 'applying the senses' (Exx 121–6) also implies a development by simplification. Ignatian contemplation is not just for beginners. Experience shows that people in different stages of development in prayer can take it up and integrate it into their own way of praying.

Contemplative: a way of being involved in the world

So far I have been looking at contemplation as a specific activity. Being contemplative, however, in Ignatian terms means more than giving time to the activity of contemplation. It is also a matter of how we engage with life and its concerns, the personal dispositions and attitudes which underlie the activity of contemplation and indeed all the activities in which we are involved. In this context being 'contemplative in everyday life' describes not so much what occupies our mind or imagination from moment to moment but rather our profounder concerns, attitudes and commitments, which give a particular flavour and direction to our lives as a whole; the things on which our hearts are set (Matt. 6:33), and where our real treasure lies (Matt. 6:21). These underlying desires and dispositions have an especially vital part to play in being contemplative in the midst of a busy life. The surface of a fast-flowing river is often broken by waves and eddies in which the water seems to rush off in all directions and even contrary to the main flow; while underneath all this busyness there is a constant, steady current which can be felt more strongly below the surface where the river is deepest.

Readers can be excused for not knowing very much about a man called Jeronimo Nadal. He does not stride like a giant through the history of spirituality yet his influence is not at all negligible.[5] Ignatius recognized him as one of the people who understood him best, and so he sent Nadal round Europe to explain the spirituality and Constitutions of the Society of Jesus to the Jesuit communities that had been recently formed. It was Nadal who noted that especially later in his life Ignatius used to contemplate the Trinity in his daily prayer and that 'Father Ignatius enjoyed this kind of prayer by reason of a great privilege and in a most singular manner'. But the next part of the same passage is far more striking and unusual: 'and this besides, that in all things, actions and conversations he contemplated the presence of God and experienced the reality of spiritual things, so that he was a contemplative likewise in action (a thing which he used to express by saying: God must be found in everything)'.[6] Ignatius as interpreted by Nadal presents a way of being contemplative in everyday life which has much to offer to Christians today.

Being 'contemplative in action' in the Ignatian sense has to do with the profounder attitudes with which we approach life and involves both surrender and commitment, two sides of love; commitment through and because of surrender. It is a surrender to God in gratitude and love which arises from the contemplation of what God is doing in and for the world and for us (Exx 230–7). The surrender involves an offering of one's gifts and talents to God to be used for the kingdom (Exx 234). And this is not simply an occasional gesture; the gesture is also a sign of a deeper, constant attitude which colours and guides all our dealings with the varied circumstances of life.

The abiding commitment which goes along with this surrender is one by which we try to give a particular direction to life and which persists within and gives shape to our particular activities. To be contemplative in daily life, in Ignatius's terms, requires a commitment to 'finding God in all things'. This means both being ready to meet God in the various forms in which everyday life reveals God to us and also, of at least equal importance, a commitment to 'finding and doing the will of God' in daily circumstances.

This does not of course mean spending one's time in conventionally 'religious' activities, though in practice such a commitment often leads people into a fuller involvement in the Christian community. It implies rather that in all the activities of daily life (looking for a job, running a family household, managing a business) and in all the choices that one makes, the basic, enduring desire is in all these things to try to be responsive to the leading of the Spirit of God (Luke 4:1), and thus in the way that one engages in life to give praise and service to God.

Signs of growth

Most people begin to be contemplative by regularly setting aside even short periods of time for prayer: this may include meditation, vocal prayer, imaginative contemplation, prayerful reading or reflection, according to what is needful or possible. These periods of prayer are the means by which we give our attention to God, a vision of the world in relation to God based on faith is appropriated, explored and deepened, and the contemplative attitudes of surrender and commitment are formed and sustained. And if scripture forms part of the basic material for such prayer and reflection, an outlook in which God is understood to be very fully engaged in the world can be developed, since this pervades the Bible from Genesis to Revelation.

In the process of coming to see and contemplate God in all things, of course, people start from different places and travel by different paths. Some are fortunate enough to grow up taking for granted even from earliest childhood that God is a benign, loving, secure, creative presence 'under the world's splendour and wonder'. Becoming contemplative for them is a matter perhaps of seeing and appreciating this God more clearly and allowing the trustworthiness of God to be a deep source of strength. Other people have more to do, because the presence and action of God in the world are far less obvious to them; or the God they know is active in the world but also demanding, perhaps even oppressive and angry, powerful but arbitrary and not at all trustworthy. For them becoming contemplative often involves more of a struggle with their images of God, and perhaps a long process of learning to find and trust a God who is fully engaged in the world for the good of individuals and of all.

Changes and development in our personal experience of prayer are related very closely to growth in other areas of life. In particular changes in prayer are linked with underlying attitudes of which we are sometimes unaware, so that what we experience in prayer is the expression and barometer of attitudes that are governing the rest of life. One usual sign of growth in a person who is becoming increasingly a contemplative in the midst of an active life is that prayer tends to become simpler. Whereas once contemplation might have involved much active work with images and busy use of the imagination in creating and responding to images, now a simple gaze at an image or a simple listening to a word in memory and imagination can be enough to hold the attention, engage the affections and evoke deeper attitudes. The image or word, whether it is in the imagination or physically, externally present, seems full of significance and attraction. It evokes and confirms underlying attitudes of surrender and commitment to God and God's kingdom in daily life. We attend to God in that image by looking, hearing, even touching and tasting, rather than by any busier use of the imagination. The image which mediates God at that moment may or may not be a conventionally religious image; any person, object or event is potentially capable of bringing us to God in this way.

Other signs of growth are linked with the interaction of prayer and the rest of life. As people become increasingly contemplative in the midst of activity, what happens in prayer gives both impetus and shape to the rest of life, and particularly to the choices that they make. Their lives begin to change. Growing familiarity with God and awareness of the presence and work of God in the world fuel the desire to collaborate with God in this saving work according to the capacity and circumstances of each. To find concrete ways of fulfilling this desire may mean changes in the shape of one's life. Perhaps more usually, the changes appear most clearly in the quality of a person's responses to events and people who are already part of his or her daily life. Contemplative appropriation of the gospel begins to colour the ways in which we live and to give our engagement in life a deeper quality of Christ-likeness.

It would be a mistake to think that the understanding of 'contemplative in action' that I have been putting forward makes setting aside time specifically for prayer redundant. For many people of course the demands of family and work make it impossible to find a time or a place for solitary contemplative prayer.[7] But being contemplative in daily life is not simply another form of a facile 'my work is my prayer', which is sometimes offered as a reason for not feeling the need to give time to contemplation, and can in fact be an excuse for avoiding God rather than an expression of a desire to find God in all things. Being contemplative in the way I have described is in fact nourished and sustained by time set apart for contemplation alone. And even at times when we do not feel a need or desire to pray, the belief that prayer is needed remains. Though the desire for God stays, deepens and grows, some people feel less need for long periods of contemplative prayer in the course of a busy life because engagement in the activities of life is not felt as taking them away from God, and shorter periods of prayer are felt to be sustaining. Because of the attitudes of surrender and commitment with which we approach them, these activities themselves bring us into communion with God; they are a share in God's own action in the world. Time set aside for contemplation is one way of being contemplative; but a full involvement in a busy life can also be another way, and people who are 'contemplative in action' learn to find God in both these different ways according to what they decide is needful and possible.

Another characteristic of growth in a contemplative approach to everyday life is increasing sensitivity to the presence and action of God in the world, and often in most unlikely circumstances. I choose the word 'sensitivity' carefully. This increasing awareness of God may often begin as a conscious effort to look for signs of God in everyday experience, in the family, at work, in television programmes or in the newspapers along with a constant commitment to find and do the will of God in all things. But the grace of God works within us to develop a sensitivity to the presence of God which is not so much a matter of conscious effort nor a process of logical argument. It becomes more part of a habitual way of seeing the world, rather like the response of a sensitive person to the presence of a friend or of a beautiful object: immediate, felt awareness and appreciation that make the contemplative person also able to reveal to others the mystery of God in unexpected places.

Along with this there grows a corresponding sensitivity to what stands or acts in opposition to God, and to the pain of others, the pain of the world. Contemplative people leading busy lives seem to develop a sensitivity to injustice, oppression and exploitation, especially when other people are the victims, and an ability to perceive these evils in places where the common opinion often is that all is well and just. This compassionate sensitivity is not only for those who are near and close but also for those who are unreached, forgotten and far away. And the characteristic response of contemplative people who are growing in this way is a compassion which constantly widens in scope, a heart which learns to exclude fewer and fewer people. Far from leading to a passive acceptance of injustice, oppression and avoidable suffering, this sensitivity gives rise to energetic action for change on behalf of those who groan in captivity and bear the yoke of oppression.

It is paradoxical too that, together with this sensitivity to injustice, people who are truly contemplative in the midst of daily life also develop a deepening serenity and inner peace. It is not the peace of ignorance, naivety or crassness. Towards the end of Ignatius's life, when the Society of Jesus was flourishing and expanding rapidly, he is reported to have said that if it were to be suppressed, fifteen minutes' prayer would be enough for him to reconcile himself with that decision and to accept it in peace. Genuine contemplatives 'in the world' are also very much in touch with the reality of the world, and its mixtures of good and evil, joy and sorrow, triumph and tragedy. But they also have certain deep convictions: that God is present and active throughout the world; that in all circumstances God works for the good of each person and of all; that far from being impeded by human weakness and poverty God expects people to be weak and frail and is happy to work with that. So rather than withdrawing from 'the world' in order to find God or passively accepting the status quo as unfortunate but inevitable, contemplative people work and pray for change: that God's glory and kingdom, present but hidden, may be more clearly seen. And this often busy and passionate work is mysteriously characterized by serenity and peace rather than anger and inner turmoil.

Discernment: integrating prayer and life

It will be clear from what I have said, especially in the last two chapters, that Ignatian spirituality involves us in a movement towards an increasing integration of prayer and the rest of life. When Jeronimo Nadal went at the request of Ignatius to explain the new Jesuit Constitutions to the members of the Society in the different European houses, the progressive integration of life and prayer was one of the continuing themes in his talks to those young Jesuit communities. Experience shows us that the circumstances of life, including apostolic ministry, draw us to prayer, either in gratitude for the gifts of God received in life or because the situations that we meet in life impress on us our need for prayer. Life reflected upon in faith is a stimulus to prayer. There is also, however, a movement in the other direction: prayer based on scripture and on the life and mission of Jesus helps us to be sensitive to the concerns of Christ in the contemporary world, to evaluate it as God does and to become engaged in that world for the sake of the kingdom of God. And this circular, integrating movement can be a feature of our Christian experience irrespective of whether we are lay people, clergy or religious, single or married, and irrespective of age and status.

The kind of contemplation that we have been looking at in this chapter is conducive to a movement towards this sort of integration. As we have seen, this way of praying does not leave us isolated from the rest of life. On the contrary it is intended to help us, in the Spirit, to see the world with new eyes, to engage us in the world and in the search to foster the kingdom of God; it is designed to change the shape of our lives in accordance with the gospel, by influencing our deepest feelings and attitudes and our most important choices. A further practice that Ignatius recommends is intended to help this process along, and that is the practice of reflecting on what happens in our prayer. In the *Spiritual Exercises* he suggests that at the end of each period of prayer the person who is making the Exercises should spend ten or fifteen minutes looking back at the time of prayer and noting what happened during that time, especially noting the 'movements', the affective experiences of 'consolation' or 'desolation' that were felt (Exx 77). The purpose of this is not navel-gazing, but to attune oneself to the leading of the Spirit not only in prayer but also in the rest of life. Outside the time of the Exercises, in the ordinary circumstances of daily life, experience shows that this practice of reflecting on what happens during prayer can be a powerful practical help towards a greater integration of prayer and life.

The form of prayer known as the 'Examen' or 'Examen of con-sciousness' is another 'spiritual exercise' that has proved to be helpful in allowing people's lives to be increasingly in tune with the Spirit of God. In the form which he describes in considerable detail in the *Exercises*, Ignatius focuses this prayer and reflection on fairly major moral defects and transgressions and 'inordinate attach-ments' which impede a person's service to God and the kingdom in obvious and significant ways (Exx 24–43). This may have rep-resented the needs of the people for whom he was originally compos-ing the *Exercises*. But this has also proved to be a powerful and necessary form of prayer even for those who take their Christianity seriously and whose lives are not characterized by blatant moral obstacles.

The principles and method of this form of Ignatian prayer are extremely simple: to look back over a given period (a day, a week, a month) and to note the significant events; and within those events to note (again) my affective responses to those events: the move-ments of feeling, of 'consolation' and 'desolation', the times when I have been drawn towards God and the service of others and the contrary times when I have been drawn away from God and wrapped up in my own selfish concerns. Once again the purpose of this is not introspection or navel-gazing but to reflect on these aspects of my daily experience, in a context of prayer, in such a way that I can be more in tune with the presence and leading of God in all aspects of my daily life.

Ignatian spirituality is a spirituality for busy people. Ignatius knew that the men who joined him to form the Society of Jesus would feel drawn towards being fully engaged in a busy apostolic life, and the clerics and lay people to whom he initially gave the Exercises were usually people much occupied in positions of influence and responsibility. Such good people tend to suffer from two opposite temptations in this matter of trying to integrate prayer and life: either to find themselves so drawn to prayer that they want to spend long hours in contemplation, with the risk that their ministry and engagement in the rest of life suffers; or to become compulsive workers, so that no time is left for prayer and the search for God's kingdom degenerates into an unreflective absorption in activity. Ignatius's approach, which is applicable to Christians in any way of life outside contemplative monasteries, is to try to move towards a balanced, discerning integration of prayer and life or ministry, such that one leads into the other and vice versa, and that there is mutual nourishment and enrichment between the two.

One of Ignatius's favourite phrases is 'discerning love' or charity (*caritas discreta*). This phrase is an attempt to capture the central feature of this integration of life with prayer. The love which draws people into engagement with life and the kingdom of God is guided and attuned to the Spirit by a habit of constant, prayerful, discerning reflection.

1 A recent helpful book on the subject of Ignatian prayer is Margaret Hebblethwaite, *Finding God in all things* (Collins, 1987). John Veltri also offers many practical helps in *Orientations*, vol. 1 (Loyola House, Guelph, Ontario, 1979).
2 cf., e.g., Exx 136–57.
3 I explored some of this territory in an article, 'Among the thorns', *The Way*, vol. 23, no. 4 (October 1983), pp. 264–72, in which I sketched a theological approach to an understanding of God's presence and action in creation, in history and in the lives of individuals.
4 cf. Exx 73–81, 229.
5 As a young man Nadal was drawn to Ignatius and his companions.

It appears that unease about Ignatius's brushes with the Inquisition and suspected association with the *alumbrados* led Nadal to take time to go away, think things over and try other possibilities before he finally committed himself later on to the Society of Jesus. We lack a good biography of Nadal. The best book on him is a theological study: Miguel Nicolau, *Jeronimo Nadal SI (1507–1580): sus obras y doctrinas espirituales* (Madrid, 1949). Joseph F. Conwell's *Contemplation in action: a study in Ignatian prayer* (Gonzaga University, Spokane, Washington, 1957) has valuable extracts from Nadal's writing on prayer and its integration in life.

6 Conwell, op. cit. p. 25.

7 Martha Skinnider is a sister of Notre Dame who for some years has been giving the Spiritual Exercises in daily life to housewives on housing estates in a deprived area of Glasgow. The only time and place for prayer many of her 'retreatants' can manage are ten or fifteen minutes in an unheated bedroom in a Scottish winter. cf. Martha Skinnider, 'Who is the Nineteenth Annotation for?' in *The Spiritual Exercises in daily life, Way Supplement* no. 49 (Spring 1984), pp. 59–69.

6

THE SPIRITUAL EXERCISES

I am sending you a book of the Exercises that it may be useful to you . . . The fact is that the power and energy of the Exercises consists in practice and activity, as their very name makes clear; and yet I did not find myself able to refuse your request. However, if possible, the book should be given only after the Exercises have been made.[1]

The Spiritual Exercises are one of Ignatius's most original and far-reaching legacies. But if you pick up the book of the *Exercises*[2] and try simply to read them, puzzlement and even boredom can soon set in, and you wonder what all the fuss is about, because for the most part, with the exception of one or two sections, they are neither interesting nor particularly enlightening to read. On the other hand, as exercises to be done with skilled guidance, experience shows over and over again that they are a powerful instrument for change and growth. Doing the Exercises involves two people whom Ignatius called 'the one who makes the Exercises' (sometimes called 'the exercitant' or 'the retreatant') and 'the one who gives the Exercises' (often called 'the director' or 'the guide'). The book of the *Exercises* is a handbook, a set of guidelines for the use of the one who gives the exercises, the director, to assist her or him to accompany the one who makes the Exercises through the process and to offer help and guidance where necessary.

The different stages of the process by which Ignatius composed the *Exercises* as we now have them are impossible to reconstruct in detail on the evidence available to us.[3] Nevertheless the basic principle of the process is clear enough. The important point to remember is that they originate in Ignatius's own personal experience, especially from the time of his convalescence at Loyola and his months in the cave at Manresa. The insights that he 'received' on one day by the banks of the river Cardoner assumed a special importance (Autobiography, 30). From an early stage he developed the habit of making notes on his experience, reflecting upon it, sifting it, interpreting it; and this process continued in later years so that he was continuously trying to understand his experience, and in particular those aspects of it that seemed to hold special significance for him at different times. His apostolic and missionary desire 'to help souls', which dates from the time of his pilgrimage, led him to find ways of using his own experience to lead others in the ways of God. It would be a mistake however to think of this as a wholly solipsistic process; naturally enough, conversations with 'spiritual' people and his reading, especially at the time of his theological studies, helped him in the process of understanding his experience and using it to help others. From the time at Manresa onwards he apparently carried around with him a sheaf of notes which he was constantly adding to and revising, and these eventually, many years later, became the book of the *Spiritual Exercises*.

The experience of the Exercises

Ignatius envisaged that the Exercises could be made and given in a variety of different circumstances and with different categories of people. This applies both to the whole Exercises and to selected exercises, whether in seclusion away from everyday occupations and concerns or in the course of daily life (Exx 18, 19, 20). But the process demands certain essential elements in any circumstances. It demands that the person who makes the Exercises does so not under any form of coercion but willingly, freely and with generosity. The generous desires with which a person approaches the Exercises, together with his or her natural abilities and capacity for spiritual growth provide a good guide to how efficacious the Exercises are likely to be (Exx 5). The Exercises create circumstances in which a meeting and communication between God and the individual person can take place, and this relationship provides the fundamental dynamic of the whole process (Exx 15). Hence the person who makes the Exercises spends several hours in prayer and reflection in the course of each day, when the Exercises are being done in seclusion over a period of thirty days (Exx 12).

The one who gives the Exercises has several functions. He or she takes care, where necessary, of the practical arrangements for food and other necessities for the person who is making the Exercises. The director also facilitates the meeting between the individual and God by briefly suggesting material for contemplation according to the plan set out in Ignatius's book (Exx 2). An essential element of the process is a regular meeting of the exercitant and the director, usually a daily meeting when the whole Exercises are being made in a month, for a conversation about what is going on in the exercitant, and especially about the movements of consolation and desolation that he or she is experiencing. In these conversations the director's role is especially to help discernment, but also to offer support and encouragement when necessary (Exx 6–14; 17). This role is the opposite of intrusive (Exx 17). The director's task is not to persuade, to give good advice, to make decisions on behalf of the exercitant nor even to influence those decisions one way or the other. The main work of the Exercises is what takes place between the individual exercitant and God: 'Therefore the director . . . *as a balance at equilibrium*, without leaning to one side or the other, should permit the Creator to deal directly with the creature, and the creature directly with his Creator and Lord' (Exx 15). The director has the privilege of accompanying and facilitating that meeting with reverence, keeping in mind too the proverb about fools and angels.

Making the Spiritual Exercises then is a complex experience involving a number of different elements. The director offers the exercitant, usually once a day when the Exercises are being made in a period of a month, material for prayer and reflection which follows the guidelines given in Ignatius's book. In the same circumstances, when the exercitant has withdrawn from everyday life in order to do the Exercises, he or she will spend four or five hours per day making the prescribed exercises, each one followed by a short period of reflection on what happened during the exercise (Exx 77). All this and the process of continuing discernment of spirits is helped by the regular, usually daily, meeting between the exercitant and the director.

Not unexpectedly, given the kind of person he was, the 'day' and its activities recommended by Ignatius have a certain structure. The periods of prayer are spaced at intervals throughout the day, with the suggestion that the exercitant might find it helpful at times and especially during the First Week to interrupt sleep to pray during the night (Exx 72). Ignatius himself prescribes the material for each of these periods of prayer or contemplation. But the material that he suggests is meant as a starting-point and he does not expect that everyone will use all the material to the same degree. The important thing in the contemplations or exercises is not to make sure of 'getting through' all the material, as if it were a syllabus for an examination, but to stay and savour whatever strikes the heart, and not to move on until one feels satisfied and ready to do so. In the course of each day it is expected that a process of focusing and simplification will take place, so that out of all the material offered for prayer and reflection, the individual exercitant gives attention to what is experienced as personally significant for him or her at any given point. Ignatius's principle here is the truth that change and growth in a person come about not so much through trying to work through a mass of material but through what strikes the heart and is grasped and savoured interiorly. 'It is not much knowledge that fills and satisfies the soul, but the intimate understanding and relish of the truth' (Exx 2). So he recommends that in the course of each day some of the prescribed exercises should take the form of 'repetitions' (Exx 62) and 'applying the five senses' to the material for contemplation (Exx 121–6).[4] This process means that the one who is making the Exercises goes over the material of previous contemplations of that day and focuses quietly on those points which have seemed particularly significant and in which consolation or desolation has been felt. Those are the points at which noticeable movements of the spirit are experienced, and they are therefore noteworthy in the process of discernment and growth.

Hence in the course of a day, then a week and then a month of this kind of activity, a pattern and a dynamic emerge which are both part of Ignatius's Exercises and at the same time particular to each individual person, just as a musician's playing of a cello concerto is both the composer's and at the same time particular to that cellist alone. In the course of this process the individual who is making the Exercises is helped to be attuned to the presence and action of God in his or her own life with its unique personal features, and from this to follow the leading of the Spirit into the future.

It is characteristic of the dynamic of Ignatius's Exercises too that in the material offered for contemplation we move from the objective to the subjective, from the revelation of what God has done and is doing, to our own and others' responses to this. So in the First Week we move from a consideration of sin at large in the world in scripture and history and social structures to, eventually but later, a consideration of our own personal sins against the background of God's love for humanity and for each of us individually (Exx 45–64). The prime focus then is God and God's self-revelation. This primary objective reference, together with the presence and help of the accompanying director, helps to prevent the process of the Exercises from becoming a purely subjective, individual experience or an emotional fantasy 'trip' with little or no grounding in objective reality.

Making the Exercises in the full form over a period of thirty days is a profound experience which affects and influences a person at different levels of the personality. As regards the overt content of the experience, by which I mean the material proposed for contemplation and consideration in the various Weeks of the Exercises, the starting point – which Ignatius calls the First Principle and Foundation – is a recognition, which is more than a notional assent, of the unconditional, creative and saving love of God for humanity as a whole and for each individual: 'men and women are created to praise, reverence and serve God our Lord, and in that way to attain salvation' (Exx 23; my translation). The recognition of the power and depth of this love is the setting in which the whole of the Exercises takes place. In a sense the unfolding of the experience of the Exercises is nothing more than the unfolding of the implications of this love in the life of the person who makes the Exercises. The more fully and profoundly one appreciates this love the richer the experience of making the Exercises is likely to be. And if a person is unable to recognize this love at the start of the Exercises it is very doubtful whether the time is right for embarking on the whole Exercises.

It is well known that Ignatius divides the material of the Exercises into four Weeks of unequal length. The length of the Weeks depends upon the judgement of the director in assessing when the one who is making the Exercises is ready to move on to the next Week, although obviously the Weeks cannot be prolonged indefinitely and the whole experience is designed to last about a month, when the Exercises are made in seclusion away from everyday life (Exx 4). After spending some days contemplating the love of God for the world, the exercitants spend more days looking long and hard at humanity's and their own responses to that love in the form of the history of sin (Exx 45–64). The purpose of this is not to induce or deepen feelings of guilt and remorse, which may already be present, but to arouse a sense of genuine sorrow for sin as a rejection of love, and even to arrive at the point of:

a cry of wonder accompanied by surging emotion as I pass in review all creatures. How is it that they have permitted me to live and have sustained me in life? Why have the angels . . . tolerated me, guarded me and prayed for me? Why have the saints interceded for me and asked favours for me? And the heavens, sun, moon, stars, and the elements; the fruits, birds, fishes and other animals – why have they all been at my service? . . . I will conclude with a colloquy, extolling the mercy of God our Lord, pouring out my thoughts to him, and giving thanks to him that up to this moment he has granted me life. (Exx 60–1)

Sorrowful appreciation of humanity's and of our own individual and collective sinful responses to God's unconditional love, and likewise of the institutions and structures in which we embody these responses, bring the one who makes the Exercises before the figure of Jesus on the cross. At this point, for Ignatius, Jesus sums up the forgiving, saving love of God for the world, expresses the scope and power of that love and also calls for a response from each of us who look upon the cross:

> Imagine Christ our Lord present before you on the cross, and begin to speak with him asking how it is that though he is the Creator, he has stooped to become human and to pass from eternal life to death here in time, that thus he might die for our sins. I shall also reflect upon my self and ask: 'What have I done for Christ? What am I doing for Christ? What ought I to do for Christ?' (Exx 53).

This movement into the Second Week already begins early in the First Week. After the profound appreciation of the disorder of sin with its tendency to enslave us and of the joyful mystery of saving forgiveness, the one who makes the Exercises is ready to look seriously at the implications of a commitment to following Jesus as a disciple, and that constitutes the bulk of the material for contemplation during the remaining three Weeks of the Exercises. The very characteristically Ignatian contemplation on the Call of the King (Exx 91–9) acts as a bridge into the Second Week and, as we saw in Chapter 3, during that Week the person who is making the Exercises is immersed in contemplating the mystery of the incarnation and the life and ministry of Jesus. The purpose of this focus is clear: 'to ask for an intimate knowledge of our Lord . . . so that I may love him more and follow him more closely' (Exx 104). This kind of love means surrender and commitment which are expressed in choices (Exx 1), and during the Second Week the exercitant spends a lot of time in various exercises, composed purposefully by Ignatius, which offer a way of exploring her or his own personal commitment to Jesus and of coming to the point of making such a commitment or renewing one already made before (Exx 135–89). Ignatius suggests that 'those who wish to give greater proof of their love, and to distinguish themselves in whatever concerns the service of the Eternal King and the Lord of all' might make this commitment repeatedly during the Second Week:

> Eternal Lord of all things, in the presence of your infinite good-

ness and of your glorious mother and of all the saints of your heavenly court, this is the offering of myself which I make with your favour and help. I protest that it is my earnest desire and my deliberate choice, provided it is only for your greater service and praise, to imitate you in bearing all wrongs and all abuse and all poverty, both actual and spiritual, should your most holy majesty deign to choose and admit me to such a state and way of life (Exx 98; cf. Exx 147).

No genuine Christian commitment can ignore the fact of the cross, though we balk at committing ourselves to sharing in the paschal mystery of death and resurrection, as did Jesus's original disciples (Mark 8: 31–33 and parallels). The Third and Fourth Weeks of the Exercises immerse the exercitant in that mystery. Again, as in the Second Week, the person who makes the contemplations of these weeks is not a detached observer of events which have only historical or academic interest. 'In the passion it is proper to ask for sorrow with Christ in sorrow, anguish with Christ in anguish, tears and deep grief because of the great affliction Christ endures for me' (Exx 203; cf. Exx 193). What befell Jesus is bound up with every disciple's own life and commitment to discipleship. The contemplations of the Third Week in particular, which focus on the suffering and death of Jesus, offer choices and challenges to anyone who makes them in the context of the Exercises as a whole. The 'meaning' of the passion and death of Jesus is neither more nor less than love without conditions. But the question they put to the person who contemplates them is whether the commitment to Jesus and the kingdom of God, made in the often headier air of the Second Week, can be sustained in the face of the cross.

In the Fourth Week of the Exercises the one who is making them moves from an experience of the cross to a share in the resurrection of Jesus and its multiple meanings for us. The gift peculiar to that Week, in Ignatius's own words, is 'the grace to be glad and rejoice intensely because of the great joy and the glory of Christ our Lord' (Exx 221). This is the point at which, also, the exercitant begins to make the Contemplation to attain Divine Love, which I have mentioned before (Exx 230–7). The Exercises began with a recognition of the unconditional, creative and saving love of God for the world and for each individual person. This contemplation allows the person who is coming to the end of the Exercises to explore the workings of that love more fully in every dimension and aspect of life. It offers a picture of the world and of human existence shot through with God's active and efficacious love of humanity. It is the vision, a new leaven – and again a surrender and commitment – with which the exercitant completes the Exercises and moves back into everyday life:

> Thus, as one would do who is moved by great feeling, I will make this offering of myself: Take, Lord, and receive all my liberty, my memory, my understanding and my entire will. You have given all to me. To you, O Lord, I return it. All is yours, dispose of it wholly according to your will. Give me your love and your grace, for this is sufficient for me (Exx 234).

A journey in freedom

Since the *Spiritual Exercises* were first published much discussion has naturally centred upon their purpose, on what exactly they are for, what they are meant to do. They have been variously seen as a way to mystical union with God; as a grounding in Christian asceticism and a fund of ascetical principles and practices; as a way of putting order into a disordered life; as a process of decision-making; as a pedagogy of life in the Spirit. Perhaps their purpose is best understood by what they actually achieve, as well as by what we know of Ignatius's own original intentions. The complexity of the experience of making the Exercises, the fact that within that experience they operate simultaneously in different areas, both conscious and unconscious, of a person's life, touching the mind, the imagination, the feelings and the most fundamental personal attitudes, choices and commitments, all this means that the actual experience is difficult to describe, especially in a few words. For many people however, in recent times, making the Exercises has meant a discovery of and a journey into an efficacious kind of personal freedom such as they have never known before. This is directly related to what Ignatius says of the purpose of the Exercises right at the beginning, in the language of his own time: 'we call Spiritual Exercises every way of preparing and disposing the soul to rid itself of all inordinate attachments and, after their removal, of seeking and finding the will of God in the disposition of our life for the salvation of our soul' (Exx 1). I want to conclude this section with a few words about growth in personal freedom.

By freedom, of course, I do not mean licence, nor do I mean the theoretical possibility, faced with two choices A or B, that we can choose B rather than A. By freedom I mean something much more like sufficient possession of ourselves so that, appreciating and relying on God's love for us, we are able to give shape to our own lives, able to commit ourselves to being the person we believe God intended us to be, and to commit ourselves to the path of life we believe God invites us, in love, to follow.

As a result of making the First Week of the Exercises, many people discover for the first time, or appreciate more fully than before, that this freedom is severely limited. There are obvious external limitations on our freedom which stem from the simple facts of physical and social living. But the experience of the First Week very often also includes the recognition of the factors within ourselves, 'areas of unfreedom' which hinder us, almost, it depressingly seems, to the point of paralysis. There are attitudes and dispositions, habits of mind and behaviour, patterns of thought and feeling, dependencies and attachments, weights and burdens from the past which trap and imprison us. That is why we need a saviour God. Blindness prevents us from seeing even the love of the God that is inviting us. Even some of our habitual and deeply-rooted images of God and of ourselves are such that they trap and enslave us rather than setting us free to be what God intended us to be. And at the present time this is true both of many who have spent half a lifetime conscientiously serving God and of others who are just beginning to do so. One of the gifts of the First Week is to be able not to despair about these distressing facts about ourselves, but to see that the unconditional, creating and saving love of God for each of us has the power to set us free from our prisons.

In the course of the other three Weeks of the Exercises the one who is making them begins to see more clearly the shape, in the following of Christ, that his or her life could have and therefore the direction in which real freedom lies. During and after the profound experience of the First Week Jesus captures the heart. On the strength of a deep appreciation of the unconditional love of God which, as I have said, should characterize the Exercises from the start, those who make them are also able to offer and commit (or re-commit) themselves in love to living as disciples of Jesus. Theirs is no blind commitment but one in which they have a realistic appraisal of their own weakness and lack of freedom (First Week), of the joy and the glory of following Jesus for love and for the sake of the kingdom (Second Week and Fourth Weeks), and of the cost that this entails in terms of poverty (Second Week) and the cross (Third Week).

Naturally it is usually in the months and years that follow the experience of the Exercises that the seeds of freedom sown here come to fruition. Thirty days is a short time measured against the slow years of human growth. What often takes place in the course of making the Exercises is a crucial change, a conversion, the beginnings of a new way of seeing and behaving whose effects have to emerge gradually in the time that follows, when we have returned to everyday life. As we have seen, this conversion and its subsequent effects are based on a profound appreciation of the presence of a loving, saving God, and perhaps new, liberating images of God to replace old, distorted ones. This also can give rise to a new image of ourselves in relation to this God which allows us to be captivated by Jesus as the first disciples were, and freely to surrender and commit ourselves in love to Jesus and the kingdom of God. Our recognition of God's unconditional love towards us as a constant, efficacious presence helps to set us free to be the people God intended us to be, less burdened and hampered by fears, guilt, anxiety and other similarly paralysing and destructive factors.

Adaptations of the Exercises

In his instructions about how to give the Exercises, Ignatius explicitly mentioned several adaptations for different circumstances and different people, as I have already said. He estimated that, for a number of reasons, not everyone would want to do or be capable of doing the whole Exercises, and not everyone who wanted to do them would benefit from them (Exx 18). Therefore, 'each one should be given those exercises that would be more helpful and profitable, according to his or her willingness to dispose himself for them' (Exx 18). And he lists the exercises which he thinks might be given to various kinds of people who would not benefit from or be capable of the full Exercises (Exx 18). Other people however, who really would profit from making the full Exercises, cannot afford the time or the money to go into seclusion away from everyday concerns for a full thirty days. So Ignatius outlines a method by which the full Exercises can be made in the course of daily life over a longer period than a month (Exx 19).[5]

Those are the main adaptations envisaged by Ignatius. The recent revival of interest in the Exercises has produced many more forms in which some of them can be given with necessary adaptations to people and circumstances. These have included adaptations in which emphasis is placed on working as a group rather than on individual guidance.[6] In his notes on giving the Exercises Ignatius emphasized the personal yet unobtrusive guidance of the exercitant by the one who gives the Exercises, through the medium of a regular one-to-one conversation. And many have found by experience that this is part of the process of the Exercises that they would be very reluctant to abandon in favour of working with a group, because it initiates a process of discernment that is outside the scope of a group. Nevertheless the group and other adaptations of the Exercises are clearly having a considerable effect for good in people's lives and are opening up some of the power of the Exercises to larger numbers of people than would otherwise be able to benefit.[7]

The one who gives the Exercises

The basic essential qualification for giving the Exercises is having made them with individual guidance from a skilled director. The experience of making the full Exercises is the school in which those who give the Exercises learn their trade. One of the skills that has to be learned, of course, is how to use the book of the *Exercises* in an appropriate way.

The book was compiled more than four hundred years ago and obviously reflects and incorporates the modes and categories of thought and language of those times, which are in many important ways different from our own. One of the temptations for some directors of the Exercises in the last twenty-five years, since Ignatius's own ways of giving them were rediscovered, has been to try to go back to the mind and practice of Ignatius in a very literal, almost antiquarian fashion, along the lines of 'this is what Ignatius wrote and did, and so we must do exactly the same'. This is not a satisfactory way of being faithful to Ignatius, just as a naive and literal application of Jesus's moral precepts, for example, is not the best way of being faithful to the gospel. Ignatius's cultural setting, like Jesus's, was different from ours. And many of Ignatius's categories of thought and forms of expression, including much of his theology, are foreign to a modern person and would not help or sustain his or her genuine growth in the Spirit if we reproduced them literally.[8] The opposite temptation lies in sitting so easy to the Exercises that what we give ceases to be recognizable as the Ignatian Exercises at all. Our perennial task is to find ways of giving the Exercises that are both true to Ignatius yet not fundamentalist, and at the same time capable of speaking intelligibly and acceptably to people of our own age and culture, so very different from those of Ignatius.[9]

For our giving of the Exercises to be both faithful to Ignatius and in the best sense 'modern', it is necessary for the directors of the Exercises to be in constant dialogue with the Exercises in their own lives and to live in constant touch with the Ignatian tradition. Perhaps the best ways to learn to give the Exercises are through this symbiosis and as an apprentice to an already skilled practitioner. But there is another point to be made. In making the Exercises we often find that our own symbols and images, which correspond to but are not identical with those which Ignatius offers, arise spontaneously. In making the meditation on Two Standards (Exx 136–48), for instance, we often find our own symbols to represent the conflict at every level of human existence that Ignatius puts in the form of two leaders with their battle-lines drawn up. This emergence of our own personal images, which are expressions of our own contemporary reality, is an important part of both doing and learning to give the Exercises: to allow ourselves and others to be immersed in the living Ignatian tradition and out of that to fashion our own images which represent in terms which we find appealing the essential truth contained in Ignatius's images and stories, as we find them in the Exercises. Adaptation to different circumstances is part of the process of making and giving the Exercises in any case, and in this form it prevents both rigid fundamentalism and its resulting petrifaction.

Conclusion

One of the greatest challenges to those people who give and make the Exercises at the present time is that of the demand and search for greater social justice, highlighted, for instance, in the theology of liberation. In the form that Ignatius left them to us, the *Spiritual Exercises* have a bias towards an individualistic spirituality. In that respect Ignatius was a man of his age. The Exercises focus on the individual person; they help an individual to find his or her own path of Christian discipleship; in the Principle and Foundation salvation, the purpose of human life is a matter of each person saving his or her own 'soul' by giving praise, reverence and service to God (Exx 23); in the First Week the sin which is the subject matter for meditation is largely the history of personal sin in others and in oneself. Not surprisingly there is no analysis of sin in terms of social structures and institutions. In the Second Week and onwards the focus is upon the individual's personal commitment to discipleship of Jesus, and apostolic mission is seen in terms of helping others to attain their own ultimate 'salvation', as Jesus did, a salvation which is seen largely in terms of future eschatology: something that happens to each individual after death.

In practice of course, outside the *Exercises* Ignatius's individualistic bias was not total. In his evangelizing, especially as Superior General of the Society of Jesus, he was concerned with those missions and projects which would produce 'the more universal good'. This in fact led him into working for social change by setting up new institutions and structures, though it is unlikely that he would have used those concepts or terms. He spent much of his time and energy establishing colleges which in fact transformed the social conditions of very many people in the places in which they were located, though they too were primarily aimed at helping people to live Christian lives and thus attain their ultimate eternal salvation.

In the text of the *Spiritual Exercises*, however, we do find an individualistic and other-worldly bias. Today a growing awareness among Christians of social injustice and oppression, and of the need for liberation from them, finds this emphasis unsatisfactory at the present time, however adequate it may have been in Ignatius's day. There is a real danger that the Exercises will form disciples of Jesus who are more or less blind to structural sin and the need for a commitment to justice as a necessary part of being a Christian. In giving and making the Exercises now we need to incorporate some new insights. We need to acknowledge that individual and personal actions inevitably have a social, structural dimension which is inseparable and unavoidable. Even activities such as prayer, which we have often assumed to be 'purely' individual and personal, are not so in fact. In our presentation of the First Week of the Exercises we need to focus quite specifically on structural and social sin as an inescapable dimension of the history of sin and as the consequence of personal sin. We must be convinced of the eternal value of all human activity. We have to see clearly that 'salvation' is not just an individual or other-worldly reality; we have a responsibility to this world that we cannot shirk if we are to be true to the gospel. The Christian disciple's commitment to Jesus cannot be a purely individual and personal matter. It has a social structural dimension and involves engaging in a struggle for a kingdom of God that is and has to be a social and political reality here and now. For 'God wills justice among people and nations in this world, so that the humanity of people is not trampled here and now even as it will not be in the final reign of God'.[10]

1   Letter of Ignatius to Alexis Fontana, 8 October 1555. The original text is in *Sancti Ignatii de Loyola . . . epistolae et instructiones*, vol. IX, p. 701, in the series *Monumenta historica Societatis Iesu*.

2   See note on terminology in Introduction, p. 6.

3   See Joseph de Guibert SJ, 'When and how the *Exercises* were written' in *The Jesuits, their spiritual doctrine and practice*, (Institute of Jesuit Sources/Loyola University Press, Chicago, 1964), pp. 113–22; and 'The authentic Spiritual Exercises of St Ignatius: some facts of history and terminology basic to their functional efficacy today', *Studies in the spirituality of Jesuits*, vol. 1, no. 2 (November 1969).

4   The nature and importance of the Ignatian 'prayer of the senses' have come in for much discussion. See, for example, Hugo Rahner, 'The application of the senses' in *Ignatius the theologian* (Geoffrey Chapman, London, 1968), pp. 181–213.

5   This is the way of making the Exercises according to the 'nineteenth annotation', which has become very popular again in recent years.

6   The 'Open Door' retreats, for instance, are based on the Spiritual Exercises but give more scope to group participation. See also John Wickham, *The communal Exercises: a contemporary version of the Spiritual Exercises in communal form* (Ignatian Centre of Spirituality, Montreal, 1989).

7   The practice of a 'preached retreat' in which the leader of the retreat addresses a group of people on the themes of the Exercises but which omits this regular meeting of exercitant and director is a development which seems to have increased considerably after the death of Ignatius. It became particularly popular out of necessity when making an annual retreat became obligatory for many congregations of religious men and women. The main weakness of this as an adaptation of the authentic Exercises is that it omits the individual, regular contact and conversation between the one who gives and the one who makes the Exercises.

8   Roger Haight outlines some of the main differences in theology between Ignatius's age and ours in 'Foundational issues in Jesuit spirituality', *Studies in the spirituality of Jesuits*, vol. 19, no. 4 (September 1987), and suggests helpful ways of moving beyond those differences in giving and making the Exercises today.

9   The problems are intensified, I imagine, when the Exercises are taken

into non-European cultures, whose thought and feeling patterns are likely to have even fewer elements in common with Ignatius, and in dialogue with non-Christian religions.

10   cf. Roger Haight, op. cit. p. 29. He suggests a rewriting of the Principle and Foundation on p. 25. On going beyond Ignatius's individualism in the Exercises, see also Jon Sobrino, 'The Christ of the Ignatian Exercises' in his *Christology at the crossroads* (SCM, London, 1978), pp. 396–424; and more radically, Juan Luis Segundo, *The Christ of the Ignatian Exercises* (Sheed and Ward, London, 1988).

7

SPIRITUAL DIRECTION

The term 'spiritual direction' often has unhappy and off-putting associations in many people's minds. It can evoke images, for example, of an authoritarian priest-confessor clandestinely telling penitents what to do and demanding more or less unqualified obedience; or of 'expert' advice given under a veil of secrecy without supporting arguments being offered for discussion. It can evoke the undesirable atmosphere of a coterie or the personal cult of a fashionable 'guru'. These and other associations are, to say the least, distasteful to people who believe in personal freedom, open discussion, consensus and democracy and who reject authoritarianism and exploitation in any form. In the recent revival of Ignatian spiritual direction it has had to be made clear that the director does not have an authoritarian or any kind of manipulative role; it is not the director's function to hold the directee in a relationship of dependency or to persuade the directee into a particular course of action, much less to impose his or her own convictions or 'way' on another person (Exx 15). The director is there to facilitate growth through discernment. In this process and in the relationship that belongs to it the personal freedom of the individual directee is very important. Ignatius's recommendation that the director should be the opposite of intrusive and like 'a balance at equilibrium' holds for spiritual direction outside as well as within the setting of the Exercises.

After looking at Ignatian discernment, prayer and the Spiritual Exercises, we are now in a better position to examine another aspect of the Christian life to which the Ignatian tradition has a valuable contribution to make: spiritual direction. At present large numbers of Christians, especially in Europe and North America, are discovering a need for spiritual direction of some kind, and books on the subject are proliferating. This rediscovery of a need for personal direction is no doubt partly due to the emphasis on individual growth which psychology and psychotherapy have maintained through recent decades. But it is also a rediscovery of a need and the corresponding skills which have been present in the Church since the early times, and which have come to prominence in various places at other periods of Christian history. The era of the monastic movement to the desert in the third century CE is a case in point.

If we go back once again to Ignatius himself and his own experience we see that especially during his pilgrimage he developed the practice of seeking out people who had the reputation of being experienced and skilled in the ways of God, in order to receive help from them. He recognized the need that he had for guidance in his apprenticeship, and went looking for help. Later on, when he became more experienced and skilled in spiritual matters, he used to engage in conversations with others in order to offer some help to them in his turn. Similarly some people whom he met and helped in this way kept in touch with him by letter, and we still have a few letters in which Ignatius offers what we would now call spiritual direction.[1]

Using particularly the *Spiritual Exercises* and some of those letters, we can attempt a sketch of spiritual direction in the Ignatian tradition. We can draw from these sources the main principles and characteristics of Ignatian direction and apply them, not now in the specialized context of the Spiritual Exercises or a 'retreat', but more generally as an element in the continuing daily lives of people who take seriously their following of Jesus.

Towards integration

The general context in which spiritual direction takes place is of course the continuous stream of events which make up daily life. We can assume that the directee is a person who wishes to take Christian discipleship fairly seriously, since he or she engages willingly and voluntarily in the process of direction. And usually, though not always, the person who looks for spiritual direction is likely to be a committed member of a Christian church or community, and regularly taking part in worship and other activities there. In this context of daily life too the directee will obviously be spending less time in prayer than when the Exercises are being made in seclusion, and is more likely to be influenced by people and by everyday currents and events.

We have seen in Chapter 5 that a movement towards a balanced integration of prayer and the rest of life is characteristic of an Ignatian approach to spirituality. We live our personal human lives in several different but interdependent and mutually interacting dimensions at once. For example our human existence has an intra-personal dimension, which has to do with our individual 'inner' selves; the intimate feelings and thoughts which occur in us and are personal to each of us. There is also a second, 'inter-personal', dimension which concerns our relationships and dealings with other individuals and groups of people; while a third dimension, the 'social-structural' dimension, points to our interactions with and participation in the social and political institutions and structures which are a constitutive part of living with other people in an organized way. Finally what might be called an 'environmental' dimension of personal living relates us to the physical, 'natural' environment which nourishes and supports human life and for which we and the whole of humanity have responsibility. I would like to stress again that these different dimensions of human existence are not separate, contiguous parts of our lives, like the divisions of an orange or the compartments of a cash box. They are more like the intermingling currents and eddies in a single stream. We exist in all of them at once, yet when we try to understand human life as a whole each of them can offer a different standpoint from which to view.[2]

Though we exist in all these dimensions at once, our experience is that at any one time only one dimension is at the surface of our awareness and the focus of our attention. The other dimensions provide, as it were, the implicit background which we take for granted and against which we attend to whatever demands our explicit attention at any given moment; rather as the lens of a camera focuses on a particular object while keeping the rest of the picture present as an unfocused backdrop to the main object. In the course of everyday life the focus of our attention constantly shifts from one dimension to another according to circumstances and the tasks we are engaged in. It may also happen that, in general terms, one or more of these dimensions receives little or no attention in the life of a particular person. A man or woman who is very much engaged in working as an activist for social change, for example, may give scant attention to his or her own personal inner life. And conversely, it may happen that an enclosed contemplative religious, unlike Thomas Merton as he grew older, sees little need for being concerned about social responsibility and political action.

Within these different currents of life our relationship with God, when we take it seriously, is not a separate compartment; rather it pervades all these different dimensions in which we live. Our dealings with God are not confined to our inner, private selves. As we have seen earlier, it is a fundamental tenet of an Ignatian approach to spirituality that God is to be met in all circumstances of life. The characteristic movement of Ignatian spiritual direction is towards a balanced integration of the different dimensions of personal existence. And the main integrating factor or principle in this process is a person's surrender and commitment to God. The steady, enduring desire to live for the 'praise, reverence and service of God our Lord', as a response to God's love for us, together with our attempts to allow that desire to give shape to our lives through our concrete choices, slowly and gradually tend to draw the multifarious elements and aspects of life into unity and wholeness.

A person who is receiving spiritual direction often finds that one dimension of his or her life in particular is a source of consolation, creativity and energy. It might be, for instance, that the friendships that I have speak to me of God and encourage me in faith and in generous openness to others. In that case one of the tasks of the spiritual director will be to support and foster that ability to 'find God' in and through relationships with others. It may also happen, of course, that a director or a directee notices that in the directee's current experience one dimension of life is hardly represented at all as a source of either consolation or desolation. Among adult Catholics in Britain, for example, the social-structural dimension is often ignored, albeit not deliberately, by loyal and devoted churchgoers, who might never advert to the fact that God's presence and action – or what is in conflict with God – might be embodied in social structures and institutions and so be a focus for prayer and a source of consolation or desolation. Not infrequently their (often unconscious) assumption is that spirituality has nothing to do with politics. In this case a spiritual director might challenge a directee by drawing attention to this apparently neglected or unrepresented dimension of life, in order to open up the road towards a deeper appropriation of the gospel and a greater degree of wholeness and integration. A director is in a position to do this as he or she stands outside the directee's own stream of life and observes it from a different standpoint.

Director and directee

In practical terms the usual setting in which spiritual direction takes place is a conversation between two people, a 'director' and a 'directee'. As in the Exercises, the role of the director is to put his or her skills at the service of the other's growth as a Christian. The conversations between the director and directee are arranged at mutually agreeable intervals, perhaps of a month or longer or shorter depending on need and opportunity. The main subject-matter of the conversation is the directee's experiences of movements of consolation and desolation in the course of prayer and everyday life in the intervening interval since the last 'session' of direction.

Many people who feel a need for spiritual direction are not in touch with these movements in their inner experience, and so one of the director's tasks at the beginning might be to help the directee to become aware of and to note this aspect of his or her personal daily experience. Movements of consolation and desolation do not take place only in a time of prayer, though in fact that might well be the time in which we are most aware of them. These states and movements of negative and positive feeling about God and God's will occur in response to many of the events and circumstances of

121

daily life, and therefore all of our daily experience, looked at from this standpoint, might be relevant to spiritual direction. What the tradition calls consolation and desolation are not so much particular parts of our total daily experience, but rather dimensions of all our experience. And what the directee brings to the spiritual direction dialogue or conversation is an account of his or her principal moments and movements of consolation and desolation in the interval since the last meeting.

The dispositions that one looks for in the directee in spiritual direction in the course of everyday life are much the same as those desirable in a person who is beginning to make the Spiritual Exercises (Exx 5, 22). If spiritual direction is to be helpful and to attain its purposes, the directee needs to be prepared to be magnanimous and generous with God, open to growth even though it is often very painful, and willing to repose trust in the director and in the guidance offered. The director needs to remember too that the main work is what happens in the living and developing relationship between God and the directee, and that the director is in the privileged position of assisting in this relationship, when called on to do so. As in the Exercises, the director's role is the opposite of intrusive. Anxiety on the director's part can sometimes lead him or her into too intrusive a position, or to too much feeling of responsibility for the shape of the directee's life and choices. It cannot be stressed too strongly that the director's role in this tradition of spiritual direction is to facilitate discernment.

It follows from this, obviously, that one of the fundamental requirements in spiritual directors is that they are in touch with the movements of consolation and desolation in their own experience and practising discernment in the course of their own everyday lives. This enables them to understand and tune into the experience of their directees, and is essential for their role as spiritual directors. This usually means that it is helpful for the directors themselves to be receiving spiritual direction from another person. But another context in which the directors can continue the process of observing and reflecting on the important aspects of their own experience, in order to be of better assistance to others, is that of the growing practice of supervision. Here the focus of attention and discussion is the directors' own experience of working as spiritual directors, and especially the significant elements and movements in that experience which occur in the course of this ministry. The role of the supervisor is to help the director to note and reflect upon this experience.

Since an uninformed or badly informed director can obviously do much harm in these circumstances, another requirement in an Ignatian spiritual director is some knowledge of theology and of the spiritual tradition of the Christian Church. Spiritual direction deals with a person's relationship with God and the ramifications in life of this relationship. This is what much of theology and the spiritual tradition are all about, and so a knowledge of them, and, what is perhaps equally important, a living, active interest in them provide a context in which the process of direction can go on with confidence. It cannot be assumed of course that holy orders (or being a Jesuit) automatically qualifies a person to be a spiritual director. A priest who has not read much theology or spirituality since he was a seminarian is not likely to be a helpful spiritual director. One of the most encouraging features of the continuing revival of Ignatian spiritual direction is the increase in numbers of highly competent lay women and men who are becoming involved in this ministry.

Another quality that one would look for in a competent director is some knowledge of human psychology, from perceptive observation of other people and how they operate as well as from study. Here a knowledge of the psychology of human development and its various stages with their typical features is especially important. With this the director has a basic understanding of how the human psyche works and the characteristics that are to be expected in people at different stages of development. This helps the director to recognize psychological problems when they occur in the directee, and lessens the chance of misinterpreting them as 'spiritual' problems and trying to apply the wrong solution. It also helps the director to understand the relationship between the psychological and spiritual in human life and growth, and to recognize the limits of his or her own competence, so as to be ready to refer a directee for professional psychological help when this is necessary.

The process

The ordinary process of spiritual direction is discernment. The director helps the directee to note and interpret the significant movements and changes in his or her inner daily experience. The director also helps the directee to move with and act upon the experiences of consolation and to endure with patience the unavoidable experiences of desolation (Exx 7, 13, 14, 317–23). In this process the directee will almost inevitably experience resistances and obstacles to the work of the Spirit within himself or herself, and, as these are sometimes unconscious, it will be up to the director gently to challenge the directee so that they come into consciousness.

Within this process the element of enabling a directee to discover and follow through in practice what seems to be his or her own personal way of following Jesus has a central place. In the mind of Ignatius this is the way to spiritual wholeness: in response to God's love for each of us, to follow one's own personal path of discipleship within and guided by the community of the Church. When we try to live in harmony with God's will in this way we grow in wholeness because our lives are increasingly in harmony with our true direction and calling. Thus Ignatian spiritual direction has to do with enabling others to find and live out a mission in the Church, in the broad sense of finding a way of living which is a response to the love God has for us and which has repercussions in the lives of other people as well as our own.

It would be a mistake, however, to suppose that this process of finding and being faithful to one's own personal path of discipleship within the Christian community is simply a matter of a once-for-all decision from which the rest flows as it were automatically; like a train which continues inevitably in the same direction along the track so long as it has locomotive power, or an aircraft flying on automatic pilot. Experience shows that our commitments do not work like that. More commonly the process of following out a personal calling has a cyclic rather than a linear shape.[3] It is a question of constantly rediscovering God's love in the different circumstances of life, and constantly re-expressing our responses to that in the concrete choices that we make. When we make a commitment to Christian discipleship it does not happen that all the different dimensions of our life immediately fall into harmony with that commitment. Through prayerful reflection on experience, discernment and spiritual direction we discover from time to time disharmonies between our central commitment and a particular aspect of our lives, it might be a certain habitual way of dealing with others, an attitude, a relationship. It is only slowly, patiently and gradually that the various parts of our lives can be brought into harmony with our commitment to God in Christ. And we do not attain perfect harmony in this life; discords and contradictions remain even in the greatest Christians to remind them of their humanity and to give hope to the rest of us. Ignatian spiritual direction has a part to play in patiently fostering, encouraging and guiding that process of bringing the different elements of life into harmony with a central commitment to Christ and the gospel.

Before ending this necessarily brief sketch of the principles of an Ignatian approach to spiritual direction, I would like to mention one other feature that is important at the present time, namely its prophetic character. We have seen that spiritual direction assists people to put into effect their desire to serve God in the following of Jesus within the Christian community. It is this desire in all things to 'praise, reverence and serve God' in discipleship that sustains and guides our search for spiritual wholeness, rather than such factors as personal ambition, the desire for social status, the search for material wealth or the need for social change. The result of this is that through Ignatian spiritual direction people are led to accept and embody in their behaviour and lifestyles values which are truly prophetic in the sense that they offer a critique of and an alternative to current social values, structures and institutions from the standpoint of the word of God. In particular, Ignatian spiritual direction is likely to make a person increasingly sensitive to injustice and oppression and to work for social change, especially in a struggle for greater justice. An effective desire for justice grows out of the integration of faith with the rest of life that is fostered by Ignatian spiritual direction.

This is in line with Ignatius's own experience and insights. We saw earlier that his own experience and pondering the gospels and the lives of the saints taught him the crucial fact that being a disciple of Jesus involves following a road similar to that of Jesus himself and adopting the values characteristic of the kingdom of God, as for example 'poverty, both actual and spiritual' as well as a willingness to 'bear all wrongs and all abuse', if that should be what God asks (Exx 98). These were the values, summed up in the beatitudes, which Jesus preached and practised as he came into conflict with the people and forces opposed to the reign of God. And they are also the values which often bring the disciples of Jesus into collision with 'what the world (in the sense of that which is opposed to and corrupts our relationship with God) loves and embraces' (*Constitutions*, 101): in Ignatius's terms, the desire for wealth, honours, status, power and pride (Exx 142). The experience of taking up one's path of discipleship, that is fostered and sustained in spiritual direction, leads a person to accept a set of attitudes and values which reflect those of Jesus. In this way Ignatian spiritual direction fosters moral and social attitudes and values which, whether privately held or publicly expressed, are recognizably prophetic within the milieu in which we live.

Towards a theological foundation

If spiritual direction fosters growth in discipleship and in spiritual wholeness through processes of discernment of spirits, the question arises as to why states of feeling and affective movements within a person's experience, which are the raw material of discernment, are in fact the foundation of growth in the Spirit. So I want to end this chapter with a brief outline of how this view of spiritual direction finds a secure grounding in theology.

I have said that the aim of spiritual direction is to help a person to (in Ignatius's phrase) 'go forward in God's service', and in the process to move towards a greater degree of wholeness and integration on the basis of a steady, efficacious desire to 'praise, reverence and serve God' in response to God's love for us. The movements and states of feeling that we call 'consolation' and 'desolation', rather than what goes on in our heads, are a sure guide to our hearts, to the deepest and most authentic truth about ourselves. (That is why affective states and movements are so important in counselling and psychotherapy too.) Our deeper affective responses to God, people and events show who we truly are, our real identity, and ultimately the direction in which our personal truth and well-being (i.e. salvation) lie. The experience of genuine consolation is an experience of being in harmony with our true selves. To move with the consolation that we experience therefore, allowing that to govern the choices that we make, promotes the growth and well-being of our true selves. The experience of desolation, by contrast, often signals that we are at odds with our true selves. When we build on our experiences of genuine consolation we are moving towards a greater degree of personal wholeness in ourselves.

We can also usefully approach this from another angle. The Spirit of God is at work within us, comforting, strengthening, leading and guiding, helping us to go forward in God's service, working to bring us into conformity with God's plan for the world and thus to wholeness. The deepest affective movements that we experience are signs of the presence and action of this Spirit in each of us. When we are in consolation we are in harmony with the work of the Spirit; when we are in desolation we are at odds with the Spirit in some way, perhaps obstructing or resisting the Spirit's action. To go along with the movements of consolation is to cooperate with the Spirit; to resist them is to resist the Spirit. Likewise to put into action the movements of desolation is to go contrary to the Spirit of God, as we experience the signs of that Spirit's action within us. And by contrast when we do not live out in our actions our movements of desolation we are making room for the Spirit to act, listening to his voice, moving towards a greater degree of wholeness.

Though I have written separately in the last two paragraphs about the human spirit and the Spirit of God, that is only for the sake of clarity and understanding. It has to be remembered that though they are two separate entities, one divine, the other human, in reality the Holy Spirit lives and acts in us in union with the deepest and most authentic desires of the human spirit. We are not two-tier creatures, with the realms of human nature and the indwelling spirit of God existing like two layers of a sandwich. The Spirit of God and our own spirit act together as one to draw us to God, to make us cry out *Abba* Father.

Discernment and spiritual direction, therefore, are powerful agents of growth. They put us in touch with the movement towards God which lies at the heart of each of us. That movement, expressed in concrete terms, includes going forward in the steady desire to praise, reverence and serve God, finding and being faithful to the personal path of discipleship to which we are called and thereby moving towards an increasingly greater degree of spiritual wholeness. This is what our hearts and our spirit most earnestly want and what the Spirit of God within us works constantly to bring about.

1   See e.g. the letters quoted in Chapter 4 on discernment, n. 3.
2   cf. *Soundings* (Center of Concern, Washington, DC, 1974); and Elinor Shea, 'Spiritual direction and social consciousness', *The Way Supplement* 54 (Autumn 1985), pp. 30–42.
3   Patrick Purnell offers a helpful cyclic model in 'Spiritual direction as a process', *The Way Supplement* 54 (Autumn 1985), pp. 3–9.

8

EMBODYING THE SPIRIT: THE SOCIETY OF JESUS

What is it to be a Jesuit? It is to know that one is a sinner, yet called to be a companion of Jesus as Ignatius was: Ignatius, who begged the Blessed Virgin to 'place him with her Son,' and who then saw the Father himself ask Jesus, carrying his cross, to take this pilgrim into his company.

What is it to be a companion of Jesus today? It is to engage, under the standard of the cross, in the crucial struggle of our time: the struggle for faith and that struggle for justice which it includes.[1]

The Society of Jesus is the principal corporate form in which Ignatian spirituality has found lasting expression. Many people who know little of Ignatius's 'spirituality', know of him as the founder of the Jesuits. But the Society of Jesus is not, of course, the only actual or possible embodiment of Ignatian spirituality. It originated and grew into its present form as a result of particular choices in response to historical circumstances. But many lay people, individually and in groups such as the Christian Life Communities, and some congregations of religious, both women and men, still find in Ignatius an attractive way of living the Christian gospel which answers their needs and aspirations.[2] In the end Ignatius did not accept women as members of the Society of Jesus, though three were admitted to profession on one occasion,[3] nor does he seem to have seen a need in his own time for a parallel congregation of female religious. Since that time however, religious congregations of both women and men have adopted Ignatian spirituality and the Jesuit *Constitutions* either wholly or in part.[4] I am going to devote this chapter to describing some aspects of the life of the Society of Jesus as one living embodiment of Ignatius's approach to Christian discipleship.

After his conversion Ignatius began to put much of his energy into expressing his personal inspirations, his experiences of 'consolation', his desires and aspirations for the service of God and others in terms of choices about particular courses of action and then in terms of the permanent structures of the *Constitutions* of the Society of Jesus. His decisions to set out from Loyola as a pilgrim, to study, to go from Paris to Jerusalem or Rome with his companions were all expressions of his desire to serve God in the best way he knew at that time. And in their own way both the *Spiritual Exercises* and the Society of Jesus as represented in its *Constitutions* are examples of attempts to give lasting expression to what he believed God wanted him and his companions to do.

His decision to found the Society of Jesus, as is well known, emerged a relatively long time after his initial conversion. Ignatius had undertaken his studies in 1524 in order to be of better service to others, and it was the same desire that led him and his companions to Rome in 1537–8 to offer themselves to the pope for the service of the Church. They made the decision to found the Society of Jesus carefully and corporately as a result of their desire to be of apostolic service to their fellow men and women and in response to the circumstances in Rome in 1538–9.[5]

When Ignatius and his companions finally arrived in Rome another controversy began. Two of them listened to a local preacher and, thinking that what he was saying showed Lutheran leanings, went to speak to him in private. This gave rise to counter-accusations and a smear campaign on the part of some disaffected former associates of Ignatius. Typically Ignatius would not rest until he and his group had been completely and formally vindicated by means of a judicial enquiry.[6] That done, Ignatius and his friends offered themselves to the pope to serve the Church in whatever capacity he wished, and the pope began to assign them to different missions both within Italy and beyond. This meant that the group of 'friends in the Lord' which had been together for some years was going to be split up. So they were faced with a choice: whether to disband and each go his own way as directed by the pope or to bind themselves into some kind of permanent group. After careful discernment together they decided to form a permanent group with Ignatius as their leader. In this way the Society of Jesus was born.

Apostolic service

'Service' is a word which occurs very frequently in the Ignatian *Constitutions* and is at the heart of Jesuit life. The founding document of the Society of Jesus describes members of the Society as wanting 'to serve the Lord alone and the Church, his spouse, under the banner of the cross'. Ignatius's and his companions' gesture of offering themselves to the pope for the service of the universal Church was a way of putting into effect the offering which each had made repeatedly in the course of the Exercises, to 'give greater proof of their love and to distinguish themselves in whatever concerns the service of the eternal King and the Lord of all' (Exx 97).[7] They offered themselves to the pope because for them he was 'the vicar of Christ on earth'. As such he had in their eyes both supreme apostolic authority in the Church and a greater concern for the needs of the universal Church and the world than any local prelate or king.

The *Constitutions* of the Society, which Ignatius was working on continuously between 1540 and 1556 in collaboration with his secretary Juan Polanco and his long-standing companions, have this strong focus on service not just in their vocabulary but in their very shape. They are not so much a 'rule' or code of law as a description of individual and corporate dimensions of the life of service in companionship that Ignatius envisaged. Parts I to IV describe the stages and processes by which a man receives his training for apostolic service, from his first introduction into the novitiate up to the time when he is ready to be admitted as a full member of the Society. Part V explains the process of full incorporation into the Society. Then Parts VI to X set out the characteristics of the individual and corporate life of this body of men given over to apostolic service. This includes chapters on the personal life of the members (Part VI); the principles by which they are to be assigned to their various forms of apostolic service all over the world (Part VII); the means by which a body so dispersed is also a united body (Part VIII); the ways in which the Society is to be governed (Part IX), preserved and developed (Part X). This final part also includes a portrait of the kind of man who would make a good superior general. From beginning to end apostolic service of men and women, undertaken and sustained out of a desire to give continuous glory and praise to God, is the primary focus and the end in view.

Discerning service

One of my contentions in this book has been that discernment of spirits is a central feature of Ignatian spirituality. Without the practice of discernment Ignatius's approach to Christian discipleship collapses. And here once again, in the matter of the Society's focus on apostolic service, continuing discernment is an instrument of primary importance. Apostolic service obviously involves making choices among various possibilities. The apostolic service which the Society offers is not intended to be at random, a matter of whim or of simply placing a Jesuit wherever someone is asked for to answer a particular need. Experience shows that not every call can be answered; any corporate entity's capacity to respond to needs is limited by countless different factors. Priorities have to be established as to where men are to be sent and for what purpose; which calls are to be answered and why.

Discernment in such matters obviously has to be both individual and communal. If the individual Jesuit makes choices about his own apostolate with little or no reference to the corporate effort, the bonds which bind the members together in one body are weakened and there is a real risk of splintering and undesirable isolation. The other extreme however, in which corporate decisions by superiors are imposed without reference to individual initiative and discernment (fortunately an increasingly uncommon happenstance these days), runs the risk of encouraging passive conformism and stifling individual contributions to the common apostolate. To maintain unity and balance, important decisions about choosing and carrying out forms of apostolic service are of necessity pondered and made both corporately and individually. For the individual member the ministries which Jesuits as a body and the local community choose to undertake provide the active context within which individuals make choices about their own ministries. This does not mean that uniformity of apostolic service – all the members of a community doing the same kind of work – is in any sense an ideal. Quite the contrary. But the Jesuit way of operating is to try to coordinate individual gifts into a communal apostolic effort with mutual enrichment and for greater effectiveness.

The 'Formula of the Institute' sets out in order of priority the kinds of ministries in which Jesuits are to be involved. Here as often in documents connected with Ignatius, there is a clear distinction between ends and means. The end is the service of faith and 'the progress of souls in Christian life and doctrine'; the rest are means:

> Whoever desires to serve as a soldier of God beneath the banner of the cross in our Society . . . should . . . keep what follows in mind. He is a member of a Society founded chiefly for this purpose: to strive especially for the defence and propagation of the faith and for the progress of souls in Christian life and doctrine, by means of public preaching, lectures and any other ministrations whatsoever of the word of God, and further by means of the Spiritual Exercises, the education of children and unlettered persons in Christianity, and the spiritual consolation of Christ's faithful through hearing confessions and administering the other sacraments. Moreover, this Society should show itself no less useful in reconciling the estranged, in holily assisting and serving those who are found in prisons or hospitals, and indeed in performing any other works of charity, according to what will seem expedient for the glory of God and the common good.[8]

Here two emphases appear: this document seems to interpret apostolic ministry primarily as service to members of the Church, though missions outside Christendom's known boundaries are also envisaged (that is, in sixteenth-century terms, among 'the Turks or any other infidels, even those who live in the region called the Indies, or among any heretics whatever, or schismatics . . .').[9] The second emphasis gives precedence to 'spiritual' ministries of word and sacrament over 'corporal works of mercy'. Part VII of the *Constitutions* proper, however, written much later at a time when Ignatius and his collaborators had had more time for reflection, allows for greater flexibility. By that time Jesuits were involved in apostolic service among non-Christians in various parts of the world as well as among members of the Church. And in the *Constitutions* Ignatius is concerned not so much to list various forms of ministry in order of priority, but to offer detailed and rather complex guidelines for a process of discernment of spirits intended to lead to a right choice of ministries and apostolates in different circumstances.[10] The guiding principle is what, among the options open to choice, will give greater service to God and to one's fellow men and women. Good discernment, here as elsewhere, involves being as fully informed as possible about one's own resources and inclinations as well as about the needs, opportunities and options within the particular circumstances in which choices have to be made and balancing them one with another.

This leads us naturally into a consideration of what a commitment to apostolic service means today for the Society of Jesus. The Society's contemporary understanding of itself is naturally grounded in the original approach to mission favoured by Ignatius and his companions, and in their conviction that they were called by God to continue the saving work of Jesus. But apostolic service also has to take into account contemporary needs, and its form is at least in part determined by those needs; otherwise it runs the risk of being irrelevant. It is after considering contemporary needs throughout the world that the Society, explicitly and as a matter of urgency, has aligned itself with the view that a genuine service of faith has to include working for justice as an integral element, an 'absolute requirement' and not an optional accessory.[11]

The mission of the Society today is the priestly service of the faith, an apostolate whose aim is to help people become more open toward God and more willing to live according to the demands of the gospel. The gospel demands a life freed from egoism and self-seeking, from all attempts to seek one's own advantage and from every form of exploitation of one's neighbour. It demands a life in which the justice of the gospel shines out in a willingness not only to recognize and respect the rights of all, especially the poor and powerless, but also to work actively to secure those rights. It demands an openness and generosity to anyone in need, even a stranger or an enemy. It demands, towards those who have injured us, pardon; toward those with whom we are at odds, a spirit of reconciliation. We do not acquire this attitude of mind by our own efforts alone. It is the fruit of the Spirit who transforms our hearts and fills them with the power of God's mercy, that mercy whereby he most fully shows forth his justice by drawing us, unjust though we are, to his friendship (Rom. 5:8–9). It is by this that we know that the promotion of justice is an integral part of the priestly service of faith.[12]

This recognition that promoting justice is an integral part of any genuine service of gospel faith lies behind the modern Jesuits' commitment to working for social change. In many areas of the world the most effective and lasting apostolic service that the Society of Jesus can offer to people, especially to those who are poor, exploited and oppressed, is to work to change those social structures that sustain the intolerable situations of institutionalized injustice, exploitation and oppression. At the present time how this commitment can be carried out individually and corporately is still a matter for discussion and exploration. For some Jesuits, working for social change becomes the leading edge or main focus of their work. The hope is that in time it will become a strong feature of every kind of apostolic service that the Society offers.

The same view that Jesuit apostolic service is service of the Church but also reaches people outside it underlies the Society's present-day commitment to ecumenism in the broad sense and to dialogue with non-Christians and unbelievers. Again for some this dialogue becomes the main focus of their apostolate, while others are still exploring ways in which an opening out to other Christian churches and groups, to non-Christian people and to unbelievers can in fact become a real dimension of numerous different forms of apostolic service.

Apostolic community

In the decades immediately before Vatican II Jesuit communities, at least in Europe, North America, India and many Latin American countries, tended to be made up of a large number (often twenty or more) of priests and brothers living in institutions of different sizes (such as colleges, universities, schools, retreat houses). In such communities it often happened that most of the members were engaged in the same kind of apostolic work within the institution to which they belonged. It was relatively exceptional for individual Jesuits to have ministries outside or unconnected with the institution. When a young Jesuit was coming to the end of his formation and about to take up active apostolic work the main question would often be which of the established institutional ministries he was destined for. And the kind of life which had evolved historically in such communities was also characteristically 'institutional', with the structures, practices, ways of forming relationships and tendencies to rigidity and uniformity which are typical of such an environment. That was how Jesuit community life had evolved after the restoration of the Society in 1814, and in that respect it was very much like other forms of religious life for both men and women.[13]

As a result of changes in the Church expressed and promoted by Vatican II, falling numbers of members in many countries, and the rediscovery of Ignatius's own desires and intentions, Jesuit community life has changed in the last twenty years. Jesuit community is more a matter of commitment than of living under the same roof. Fostered and guided by the experience of the Exercises, Jesuits make a commitment to God and to Christ, to serve 'under the standard of the cross' in apostolic mission. This also involves a commitment to spend one's life as a fully participating member of a particular group of people, the Society of Jesus. When he makes his profession the Jesuit is incorporated into a worldwide body of men numbering at present about 25,000. In practice for most of them however, their commitment engages them to be part of a particular 'province' and to share its life, fortunes and work.

Naturally Ignatius's own experience coloured his concept of Jesuit community. He had spent years as a solitary, penniless pilgrim, an equally needy student and then as one of a small band of 'reformed' wandering evangelists. He expected that Jesuits would be frequently on the road, scattered in a diaspora; and any understanding of community has to include the fact of dispersion and the threat that this poses to unity. Jeronimo Nadal put this element of mobility in somewhat extreme terms and images which time has tempered:

> They realise that they cannot build or acquire enough houses to be able from nearby to run out to the combat. Since that is the case, they consider that they are in their most peaceful and pleasant house when they are constantly on the move, when they travel throughout the earth, when they have no place to call their own, when they are always in need, always in want – only let them strive, in some small way to imitate Christ Jesus, who had nowhere to lay his head and who spent all his years of preaching in travelling.[14]

At the same time it is important to remember that Ignatius hardly moved out of Rome between 1540 and 1556, and consequently by the time he was writing the *Constitutions* the experience of living in and building a resident Jesuit community was being added to those of being a wanderer. Moreover as superior general of the order he had the task of holding together and developing a worldwide network of scattered individuals and groups, mainly by the many letters he wrote. He also gave detailed instructions for the establishment of other permanent Jesuit communities and colleges in Rome and elsewhere. These experiences and demands meant that Ignatius and his collaborators had to develop and articulate a concept of community which would both express their apostolic aspirations and relate directly to the circumstances in which Jesuits were living. So Ignatius recognizes in the *Constitutions* both the threat that comes from dispersion and other factors on the one hand (Part VII) and on the other hand the corresponding need to maintain an effective commitment to unity and community (Part VIII):

> The more difficult it is for the members of this congregation to be united with their head and among themselves, since they are so scattered among the faithful and among unbelievers in diverse regions of the world, the more ought means to be sought for that union. For the Society cannot be preserved, or governed, or, consequently, attain the end it seeks for the greater glory of God unless its members are united among themselves and with their head.(*Constitutions*, 655)

For Jesuits it is their commitment to God, to apostolic service, to the members of the whole Society and to each other that forms the basis of community, rather than some external uniformity or living under the same roof. In the light of this the local Jesuit community is a particular, and often transient, embodiment of their common commitment:

> Moreover, it is in companionship that the Jesuit fulfils his mission. He belongs to a community of friends in the Lord who, like him, have asked to be received under the standard of Christ the King. This community is the entire body of the Society itself, no matter how widely dispersed over the face of the earth. The particular local community to which he may belong at any given moment is for him simply a concrete – if, here and now, a privileged – expression of this worldwide brotherhood.[15]

Seen in this way Jesuit community not only offers but even demands the possibility of different forms of lifestyle. The primary focus, as always, is apostolic service and its requirements, which in a particular instance may imply that Jesuits live singly, in a small group, in a scattering of small groups and individuals living alone or in a large group in an institutional apostolate. The kind of lifestyle that is chosen is a matter for deliberation and discernment, which will usually mean, once again, balancing in due proportion the demands of the apostolic situation, the personal needs and desires of the individual people concerned and any demands that the Society as a body might wish to make. This is likely to result in a variety of lifestyles in any one province. The needs of Jesuit college students, for instance, differ from those of a parish team, retreat centre staff or college faculty. In addition ways of relating to each other and of organizing communal living are likely to vary according to the size of the community. Moreover it is increasingly common now to find Jesuit communities made up of members with different kinds of apostolic work, and their individual and common needs have to be respected.

At the present time signs of a commitment to community among Jesuits are many and varied. They are no longer such things as uniformity of dress or a common daily timetable and apostolate, external features which have never been absolutely reliable signs of a common commitment to unity. Much more significant indications are such things as effectively offering mutual affection, support and companionship; a willingness to spend time with one's immediate local community and to put one's energy into praying together, contributing to meetings, cooking and doing housework, relaxing and going on holiday together; and outside the immediately local grouping, being willing to participate in province and international projects and meetings, committees and working groups, answer questionnaires, write for the newsletter and so on, all very often at some considerable personal inconvenience. In addition, since Jesuits are always scattered through the world, keeping in touch by letter and phone is also a sign of a commitment to community, to what Ignatius called the 'union of hearts' (*Constitutions*, 655).

It will be clear from this that there is an inescapable tension in Jesuit life between apostolic service and community. One pole of the tension is the demands of apostolic service, the other the commitment to community. Obviously individual Jesuits experience the tension in different ways according to personality and temperament: some are drawn strongly in the direction of apostolic work, while others are more naturally 'homemakers', and others again seem to exhibit very definite 'loner' or eremitical tendencies. Within this inevitable tension Ignatius's own emphasis is pretty clear: apostolic service takes priority. But the tension has to be maintained rather than disposed of by the elimination of one of its elements, for without the commitment to community there is little meaning in belonging to the Society; a man might as well be a freelance evangelist.

Obedient men?

For a long time Jesuit obedience in the popular imagination has been taken to mean a strict, even rigid, unquestioning, militaristic discipline. Though this is a distorted picture both of Ignatius's concept of obedience and of present-day practice, much of what Ignatius wrote about it leaves the impression on our minds at least of an authoritarian man. That is not wholly surprising. His was an age of belief in the divine right of kings; the society on which he grew up was feudal, with a relatively fixed hierarchical structure, and his family was used to command as well as to obey. The democratic ideal, offering greater chances of both upward and downward mobility, had yet to make its advances in European politics, let alone the Church. Consistent with his age Ignatius saw authority in the Church and the Society of Jesus as given from above: the pope, as the representative of Christ on earth, Ignatius held as having authority over the Society and all its members, especially as regards doctrine and mission. For him it was from Christ and through the pope as head of the Church that superiors in the Society received and exercised authority within their own limits. And Ignatius encouraged members of the Society to obey their superiors with the reverence they would give to Christ himself, since they stand in his place. When writing about obedience he uses terms such as 'instruments' in the hand of God, 'obedience of will and judgement' and 'blind obedience', as well as the traditional images of 'the dead body' or the 'old man's staff' which allow themselves to be carried from place to place and used in any way whatever.[16] Understandably these images have sometimes been read as implying that obedience means supine passivity, abandonment of all personal initiative and responsibility, a reduction to the status of an infantile pawn.

In practice the obedience that is part of Jesuit life and an expression of key elements of Ignatian spirituality implies a two-way relationship, in which, ideally, openness and friendship have an important part to play. For Ignatius, in order to be effective, the collaborative relationship of authority on the one hand and obedience on the other presupposes on both sides a willingness to work together in discernment. It is not a matter of one person in authority telling another what to do without reference to that person's gifts and inclinations, and demanding unquestioning 'blind obedience'. The individual Jesuit recognizes and accepts the fact that a superior has the final say in assigning him to an apostolic mission and in other aspects of his life. But for that to be effective it presupposes first that the individual Jesuit is practising discernment of spirits as an element in his own daily life, so that he is aware of his own gifts and inclinations, his strengths and weaknesses and the areas in which he finds encouragement or discouragement, consolation or desolation. It also presupposes that the individual is willing and able to reveal these movements of feeling to the superior, so that the person with whom the decision finally rests is actually aware of 'how he feels'. And a third requirement of effective obedience of this kind is that the superior is willing and able to listen openly and freely to what the individual has to say and to take it into account in coming to a decision. This is not therefore an infantile relationship of child to father nor a supine passivity which by-passes the exercise of freedom, but an interaction between two adults involving openness, discernment and mutual affection.

That is the context in which Ignatius's often stark words on obedience have to be read. His originality was to make this relationship of openness and common discernment the principle and foundation of government at every level throughout the order.

For this obedience to work both corporately and individually, Ignatius wrote into the *Constitutions* guidelines for the practice of what is called 'manifestation of conscience'. This was originally intended to be a characteristic feature of Jesuit life, and its importance has once again been recognized in the recent 'rediscovery' of Ignatian spirituality.[17] For Ignatian obedience to be successful the superior should have as complete a knowledge as possible both of the circumstances of the mission and of the individual Jesuits who are assigned. Otherwise it is likely that the wrong man will be put in the wrong place; men will be assigned to tasks which are outside their powers; apostolates will be undertaken which cannot be maintained and serious injustice will be done to those people whom it is intended to serve.

The Society of Jesus started life in an ethos of open discussion and affection characteristic of a group of 'friends in the Lord', and this, not military discipline, is supposed to characterize Jesuits' dealings with each other even now. The practice of 'manifestation of conscience' means that the individual Jesuit undertakes to reveal in confidence to his superior, usually annually but more often for those still in 'formation', his personal attitudes and feelings, his movements of 'consolation' and 'desolation', in fact whatever is going on in his own life that he feels is relevant to his personal growth and to carrying out the apostolic service to which he is assigned. This is a necessary contribution to the kind of decision-making and government at every level that Ignatius wanted. Its aim is to make service of God and others more effective by uniting the members of the Society among themselves and allowing them to take up those forms of apostolic ministry to which they are drawn and for which they are suited, within the setting of the Society's corporate apostolic effort.

Preaching in poverty[18]

When Ignatius was writing the chapters on poverty in the Jesuit *Constitutions* several images from his earlier experience can be seen to have influenced him strongly. Two of these are the figures of the pilgrim and that of the travelling evangelist who went about from town to town and village to village much as Jesus himself had done in his own ministry. But as we have seen, even within Ignatius's own lifetime Jesuits were not simply wandering preachers with no fixed abode. Communities and colleges were established, the Society developed from a travelling band of companions into a worldwide body with several different provinces and increasingly complex structures. Any expressions of evangelical poverty had to take account of those changes.

Ignatius seems to have written the *Constitutions* under the influence also of one of his most important, though not original, insights about the gospel, namely that taking Christian discipleship seriously involves accepting and even desiring poverty as a way of being aligned with Jesus (Exx 98, 116, 146–7). In this sense poverty is in the first place a theological idea rather than an economic or sociological one. Jesus became poor in that he rejected the way of self-assertiveness, self-interest and power and gave himself over to others in service and self-forgetful love, which led eventually to the extreme poverty and helplessness of the crucifixion. We have already seen how big a part this poverty and *kenosis* of Jesus played in Ignatius's understanding of Christian discipleship.

This approach to evangelical poverty finds expression in various ways in the lifestyle and structure of the Society of Jesus. There is first a sharing of goods and resources in a form of common life. In the vow of poverty each member of the Society offers himself and his gifts to the Society as a whole and to its members, and through apostolic service these resources are also shared more widely with others. The goods that are shared are obviously very various and include material resources alongside time, energy and other individual gifts and abilities. This sharing of goods is an embodiment of a desire to put one's resources, individually and corporately, at the service of others for the sake of the gospel. It gives concrete expression to the offering made in the Contemplation to Attain Divine Love: 'Take, Lord, and receive all my liberty . . . all that I have and possess . . .' (Exx 234).

The same desire also lies behind Ignatius's intention that the Society of Jesus as a body, and individual members when called upon, should be characterized by a mendicant type of poverty. That is, they should offer their apostolic service free of charge, 'giving gratuitously what they have gratuitously received' (Matt. 10:9).[19] In order to incorporate this into the permanent structure of Jesuit life Ignatius wrote into the *Constitutions*, after much careful heart-searching and discernment (which is charted in his spiritual diary), the proposal that houses of 'professed' Jesuits, which in practical terms means all those houses which are not devoted mainly to the training of Jesuits 'in formation', should have no permanent revenues, as, for example, from land or endowments (*Constitutions*, 553–65). Instead, once their period of training was over and they were involved in apostolic work, Jesuits should live more obviously from hand to mouth, being supported by what they received in alms and offerings for their ministry.

For a large body of people with a complex worldwide organization to practise effectively a mendicant type of poverty at the present time is not a simple matter, however strong the desire. Even though the number of Jesuits had risen sharply before Ignatius died, he was still dealing with far smaller numbers than the modern Society and a social order with simpler economic structures than our own. And in modern times the practice of a mendicant poverty such as Francis and Ignatius envisaged it is made more difficult by the fact that the general population is no longer made up of Catholics who see the point of evangelists being supported by alms. Nevertheless Ignatius's intentions about corporate and individual poverty still stand, and the Society as a body is constantly trying to put Ignatius's concept of evangelical poverty into the concrete terms of financial organization and effective apostolic service in continuously changing and very complex economic conditions.[20] This choice of gospel poverty, and its expression through sharing of resources, common life of a fairly simple kind, along with gratuitous apostolic service, constitute another aspect of the prophetic quality of Ignatian spirituality, especially in a time of materialism and consumerism.

The Society of Jesus's response to the Church's call for a 'preferential option for the poor' is another dimension of gospel poverty, and very definitely within the authentic tradition of the Ignatian approach to discipleship. It is an apostolic commitment to stand on the side of poor and oppressed people, to offer them loving service, to be when necessary the voice of the voiceless and to work to change the social institutions and structures which sustain poverty, injustice and exploitation. An option for the poor is first and foremost an attitude of the heart, a form of love which finds expression outwardly in concrete choices about lifestyle, community and especially apostolic service. It is another flowering of a desire to continue the ministry of Jesus who aligned himself especially with marginalized people (Mark 2: 15–17 etc.), surprisingly pronounced them blessed (Luke 6:20ff) and spent his time ministering among them. Within the Society of Jesus there is ample room and freedom to live out a preferential option for the poor in a variety of ways. For some Jesuits it means choosing actually to live and work among the very poor, sharing the same conditions of life as fully as possible, so as to demonstrate God's preferential love in an easily recognizable form. Others who feel that they do not have the means to build that particular tower (Luke 14:28ff), none the less want the same attitude of heart to permeate and give a definite colouring to all the different forms of apostolic service that they have to offer: education, the Spiritual Exercises, work with young people, research, refugee services, theological reflection, parish ministry and so on. How to do this effectively is something which Jesuits, corporately and individually, are still struggling to learn.

The break with monasticism

It will be clear from what I have said about the Society of Jesus that Ignatius's concept of a religious order represents a break with the monastic tradition of religious life. Even the Franciscans and Dominicans, whose emphasis was more clearly apostolic than that of the monastic orders, had and still have conventual elements – chapter government and Divine Office in common, for example – that Ignatius was not willing to adopt. Whereas the monastic orders gather people together as a community to serve God by prayer, liturgy, study and manual work in the monastery, Ignatius envisaged his men being able to respond to needs in any part of the world and hence living in a diaspora for the sake of apostolic service. And, as we have seen, his concept of mendicant poverty, regulated by the demands of apostolic service, was more akin to a Franciscan than to a monastic ideal.

Ignatius's break with the monastic tradition is also evident in his understanding of the kind and amount of prayer appropriate for

Jesuits. The Jesuit vocation is undoubtedly a contemplative vocation, but in a rather specialized sense: 'For while it is "in action" that we are called to be contemplative, this cannot obscure the fact that we *are* called to be contemplative'.[21] Hence Ignatius himself and many of the subsequent official documents of the Society put strong emphasis on 'familiarity with God' in personal prayer and the continuous effort to integrate prayer, ministry and the rest of life, so that God is found 'in all things'.

While the *Constitutions* stipulate the amount and kind of prayer thought suitable for Jesuits in the years of their study and formation (26, 342–5, 582–5), those who are professed and engaged in apostolic work are given the freedom to arrange for themselves, in consultation with the superior and their spiritual director, the pattern of regular prayer that is appropriate for them individually. That is because 'it is presupposed that they will be men who are spiritual and sufficiently advanced to run in the path of Christ our Lord to the extent that their bodily strength and exterior occupations undertaken through charity and obedience allow' (*Constitutions*, 582; cf. 582–5).

As with other areas of life personal prayer is a matter of continuing discernment for the individual Jesuit, and both the length of time he regularly spends in prayer and the kind of prayer he finds helpful are likely to vary with changing circumstances and at different periods of his life. The underlying presupposition is that a person called to be 'contemplative in the midst of daily life' might consistently feel a need and a desire to pray, or, when that desire is lacking, will believe that prayer is, if anything, the more needed. That this variety in time and styles of prayer should be possible is an integral element of Jesuit life. And to allow for greater flexibility in their apostolic service, Ignatius would not have Jesuits committed to reciting, let alone singing, the Divine Office in common, though Jesuit priests have the same obligations towards the Office as diocesan priests. At the present time too most Jesuit communities have a short period of prayer in common daily or several days a week, but the pattern varies greatly from place to place.

The same flexibility and freedom are offered with regard to the ascetical practices usually associated with religious life, especially in monastic traditions (*Constitutions*, 582). The demands of apostolic service and community, balanced by the necessity for appropriate relaxation and leisure, provide the fundamental pattern of asceticism and discipline. If an individual Jesuit wishes to take up other ascetical practices over and above these he does so in consultation with the superior and his spiritual director. The principle here as elsewhere is that of 'discerning love' (*caritas discreta*). Ascetical practices which disable a person for apostolic service and the demands of community, injure health or preclude necessary recreation are discouraged (*Constitutions*, 580, 582–3).

There is obviously much more that could be said about the Society of Jesus and its way of life. From this however it is clear that the elements of its life, its structures and practices and the lives of its members embody some of the most important features of Ignatian spirituality, always of course with the limitation that being human imposes on our ability to realize ideals. At the heart of Jesuit life, as with Ignatius himself, there is discernment of spirits, within the context of a living devotion to the person of Jesus and a desire to follow him in apostolic service. This is fostered by making the Spiritual Exercises, which Jesuits do twice in their lives, and by an annual retreat of eight days in which there will be resonances of the Spiritual Exercises. The *Constitutions* offer structures and practices designed to make this way of apostolic service according to the mind of Ignatius possible for the Society as a body and for individuals within it. The daily life of the Society represents its attempts to be constantly faithful to the gospel, to the Church and to its mission within the changing circumstances and challenges of history.

1 Decrees of General Congregation 32, decree 2, nos 1, 2.
2 The Christian Life Communities are a worldwide federation of groups and communities of lay Christians whose spirituality is Ignatian.
3 This story is told briefly in, e.g., Dalmases, op. cit. pp. 90, 254–5.
4 At the beginning of the seventeenth century Mary Ward, an Englishwoman and founder of the Institute of the Blessed Virgin Mary, believed that she and her nascent Institute should adopt the

Constitutions and way of life of the Society of Jesus, but she was opposed in this by the Church authorities and did not succeed. See Lavinia Byrne, *Mary Ward: a pilgrim finds her way* (Carmelite Centre of Spirituality, Dublin, 1984). More recently different branches of Mary Ward's Institute and other women's religious congregations such as the Faithful Companions of Jesus and the Irish Sisters of Charity have been able to adopt the Ignatian *Constitutions* and way of life more fully.

5   cf. Jules J. Toner, 'The deliberation that started the Jesuits', *Studies in the spirituality of Jesuits*, vol. 6, no 4 (June 1974).

6   Dalmases, op.cit. pp. 157–63, gives the facts briefly. One of the surprising features of the arrival in Rome of this band of 'reformed priests' is the fact that Ignatius seems to have had almost immediate access to the pope as well as to various cardinals. Perhaps his earlier service at the courts of the Chief Treasurer of Castile and the Duke of Nájera opened doors to him which were closed to others. And it was characteristic of Ignatius to use whatever influence he could legitimately muster.

7   The Jesuits' 'fourth vow' of obedience to the pope has its origin here. It is one way of making effective the commitment to share in the mission of Jesus in the service of the kingdom, the world and the Church.

8   'The formula of the Institute', s. 3, in *Constitutions*, pp. 66f.

9   ibid. s. 4, in *Constitutions*, p. 68.

10   *Constitutions*, pt VII, chs 1, 2 (603–32).

11   General Congregation 32, decree 4, 'Our mission today', s. 2. Sections 24–7 of the same document offer a survey of present-day worldwide needs which call for a commitment to justice.

12   ibid. s. 18.

13   John Padberg has written a short history of Jesuit community, 'How we live where we live', *Studies in the spirituality of Jesuits*, vol. 20, no. 2 (March 1988). General Congregation 31 set out guidelines for modern Jesuit community living in its decree 19, and these were endorsed and developed by General Congregation 32 in its decree 11 on 'The union of minds and hearts'.

14   *Monumenta Nadal*, vol, V pp. 773–4 in the series *Monumenta historica Societatis Iesu* (Jesuit Historical Institute, Rome).

15   General Congregation 32, decree 2, ss 15–16.

16   cf., e.g. *Constitutions*, nos 84, 284, 286, 342, 424, 547, 551, 552, 618, 619, 627, 661, 765. It is important that we read Ignatius's famous 'letter on obedience' (*Letters*, pp. 287–95) in its proper context, as a response to a particular critical situation and not as the last word on Ignatian obedience, valid for all times and places. There is evidence in the letters too that Ignatius's thinking on obedience developed as he watched the Society of Jesus grow from a band of friends into a worldwide organization with about 1000 members by 1556.

17 The obligation of 'manifestation of conscience' and the reasons for it
    are set out in the General Examen, nos 34–6; cf. *Constitutions*, pp 103–4.
18 For a fuller discussion of Ignatian poverty see Michael Ivens, 'Poverty
    in the Constitutions and other Ignatian sources', *The Way Supplement*
    61 (Spring 1988), pp. 76–88.
19 cf. *Constitutions*, 565; 'Formula of the Institute, ss 3, 5, in *Constitutions*,
    pp. 67, 69.
20 The Society of Jesus's struggle to live poverty effectively and faithfully
    in today's world is reflected in decree 18 of General Congregation 31,
    decree 12 of General Congregation 32. Regular revision and updating
    of the *Statutes on poverty* are a continuing attempt to express Jesuit
    poverty in terms of more particular legislation.
21 General Congregation 32, decree 11 on 'Union of minds and hearts',
    s. 8.

9

IGNATIAN SPIRITUALITY AND THE CHURCH

Ignatian spirituality, as I have presented it, involves a focus on the individual person in his or her following of Jesus. This focus is natural in the circumstances because much of Ignatius's legacy to us concerns ways of understanding and handling on an individual basis the processes of conversion, discernment, choosing, commitment and growth which take place in the lives of individual people. That is not to say however that Ignatian spirituality ignores the community and social dimensions of the Christian life. In Chapter 8 we saw that Ignatius's *Constitutions* for the Society of Jesus are an outline of a corporate, structured way of being a Christian. And Christian discipleship in its integral form is discipleship in a community of faith. Attempts to be a disciple of Jesus and to try to live the Christian life apart from a community of faith do not in the end make sense. Ignatius took it for granted that anyone whose life was influenced by the Spiritual Exercises would want to live as a member of the Church, which for him meant the Roman Catholic Church, which was then in the crisis of the Reformation. The later Ignatian tradition of spirituality envisages living the Christian life as a member of a Christian church community.

Ignatius's own concept was of the Church as a hierarchical and monarchical institution, and in this he belonged firmly to his own age.[1] His ideas and our own about what the Church is and about the existence of a multiplicity of Christian denominations, groups and communities would inevitably differ considerably. We live in a different age from his, our theological understanding of the Church has developed greatly since his time, and our ecumenical attitudes and thinking have changed through theological reflection on the vagaries of history. None the less, whatever Ignatius's own views were about the reformed churches, a notable feature of Ignatian spirituality at present is that it has crossed boundaries between different Christian denominations. It thus offers a fruitful ground for developing ecumenical dialogue and collaboration.

Such a complex reality as the Church cannot be described in a few words. We do have at our disposal, however, many 'models' or images which help us to understand more clearly what this complex reality that we call the Church is. No single one of these images by itself is enough to describe the Church, but together they bring out different important aspects of the nature and purpose of the Church and its relationship to the rest of human reality which we call 'the world'. So we find images of the Church as a communion, a community of faith, a hierarchical institution, the people of God, the body of Christ, the spouse of Christ, a herald of the good news, a servant, and these are only a few images among many in scripture and Christian tradition. Each makes its own contribution to an integral picture of the Church, and each has both strengths and weaknesses.[2]

The Ignatian tradition as it exists today is at ease with several different models of the Church, and does not adopt any one image as exclusively significant or enriching. That is not to deny that some models are more helpful than others. A wide range of people from a variety of Christian churches and communities who occupy different positions on the spectrum of images of the Church are at present discovering a resonance with an Ignatian approach to Christian living. None the less, what I propose to do in this chapter is to outline a basic image of the Church which seems to me both to cut across some of our denominational boundaries and to be in close harmony with our tradition of Ignatian spirituality.

The Church: a community at the service of the world

The image of the Church as 'servant' of humanity and of the world is a fairly recent development, which was stimulated by Vatican II.[3] It is an image which stresses first the fact that the Church is not just an institution with a hierarchical structure but also, and more appealingly, a community of believers who are united by the bonds of a common faith, a shared hope for the future and love for one another. It also points to continuity between the role of the Church and the mission of Jesus the Son of man who came 'not to be served but to serve, and to give his life as a ransom for many' (Mark 10:45).

The Church is at the service of the world because each human being without exception is called to fulness of life in Christ, and the Church is at the service of humanity in a search to realize this call for each and every person. The images of 'servant' and 'service' are also important in that they highlight the kind of relationship envisaged between the Church and the world. The Church is called to offer itself and its resources to humanity by 'taking the form of a servant' (Phil. 2:7), humbly, reverently and with love, eschewing triumphalism, domination and the way of self-assertive power. According to this image of the servant, the Church fulfils its purpose when it serves to promote the best interests of humanity, not by standing apart but by entering fully into the human condition and from that standpoint offering to show the way to fulness of life in Christ. We know that we will only finally reach the completion of this in the life of the world to come, but that does not mean that this world and its concerns are unimportant or negligible and that we should have our eyes fixed only on the future kingdom. This life is a preparation for, a movement towards the final fulness; it is the context in which we work out our salvation, and consequently no aspect of this life is negligible; everything makes a contribution to the journey towards fulness of life in Christ. That is why the Church, as servant of the world, cannot neglect ordinary human concerns. It is called to put its material, intellectual, social and spiritual resources at the services of the deepest aspirations and the well-being of humanity in all its various dimensions, economic, political, artistic, scientific as well as moral and religious. Whatever is human is the concern of the Church.

The Church: a community at the service of the kingdom

Another aspect of the servant image of the Church is the fact that the Church exists to serve the kingdom of God. The Church is not identical with the kingdom of God; the kingdom exists outside the boundaries of the Church, wherever God is present and active. The role of the Church is to disclose the kingdom to those who are looking for it, to put its resources at the service of establishing and sustaining the life of the kingdom. In other words the Church exists to call attention to the kingdom of God and to work to enable God to reign in every corner of human life. Here too the Church is continuing the mission of Jesus, who told people 'the kingdom of God is very near to you' (Mark 1:15) and backed this up with signs which disclosed the presence of the reign of God in every dimension of human life.

It is likewise true to say that the reign of God will only reach its fulness in the life to come. But it is equally true that 'our God reigns' here and now, the kingdom exists among us, though in an incomplete form. Nor should the reign or kingdom of God be thought of in dualistic terms as 'spiritual' as opposed to 'material' Like the leaven in the dough (Matt. 13:33) the reign of God reaches into every level of human life, material, social, political, artistic, scientific, intellectual, psychological and emotional as well as religious and 'spiritual', and the Church's call is to serve the kingdom at all those different levels. No aspect of human existence is irrelevant to the kingdom of God and therefore no aspect is irrelevant to the service which the Church is called to offer.

It is easy to see how this image of the Church as servant is in harmony with the central elements of Ignatian spirituality. Ignatius's laconic but pregnant statement that men and women are created to praise, reverence and serve God and in that way to attain salvation (Exx 23) reflects his view of the whole of humanity coming from God and being called to fulness of life with God. And, as we have seen, his picture of the incarnation stresses the universal scope of the mission of Jesus, as the 'Three Divine Persons' look down from their throne upon 'the whole expanse or circuit of all the earth filled with human beings' (Exx 102), and plan 'to work the redemption of the human race' (Exx 107). Moreover, when Ignatius was sending Jesuits out across the world, they were not concerned with simply maintaining the institution of the Church by providing services for those who were already members. On the contrary they were reaching out among non-Christian people in the hope of preaching the good news and showing the way to fulness of life in Christ. Nowadays of course we would balk at and disavow some of the assumptions that Ignatius and the early Jesuits made about the spiritual state of non-Christian people – 'all nations in great blindness . . . descending into hell' (Exx 106) – and at some of the 'missionary' methods they used. There has been genuine development in these areas, which does not alter the fact that a perception of a universal call to fulness of life in Christ and of the Church at the service of that call is a genuine part of the Ignatian spiritual tradition.

The view that the kingdom of God touches anything that is genuinely human and that the Church is at the service of this kingdom is reflected in the fact that in their apostolic service Jesuits and others who follow Ignatius do not concern themselves only with what is specifically or obviously moral, religious or spiritual or with pastoral ministry within the Church. In the face of multiple needs choices have to be made, and a central question in discernment is always, 'How would Jesus react in these circumstances?' The answer to this leads people into engagement with every human need according to what different circumstances demand: providing fresh drinking water in Indian villages; feeding, clothing and sheltering refugees; working for the liberation of poor and oppressed people in Latin America; doing social work in inner-city areas of Europe and North America; teaching and doing research in science, technology, media, literature, political and social science, philosophy and arts in every corner of the world, as well as in theology; stimulating and sustaining dialogue with members of non-Christian religious groups or with unbelievers. All this and so much more is grounded in the conviction that the kingdom of God and the Church's service of the kingdom touch every possible dimension of human life.

The Church: context for discipleship and service

Whatever images of the Church one adopts, one of the most important functions of the Church for those who follow the Ignatian
approach to spirituality is to provide a context for discipleship,
mission and apostolic service. Ignatius himself was an evangelizer.
The Church has a mission to evangelize, to serve the kingdom of
God and to lead people to fulness of life in Christ. The missions
of individuals and groups within the Church are obviously part of
that wider mission of the whole Church, and all contribute to the
continuation of the saving work of Jesus.

This means that the community of the Church is a community
of disciples of the Lord which nurtures and sends individuals and
groups for apostolic service, both to serve the members of the
Church and to reach out to those who are not visible members. So
it was that Ignatius and his companions decided to offer themselves
to the pope as the leader of the worldwide Church, envisaged
missions from the pope as part of Jesuit life (*Constitutions*, 603–17),
and stipulated that members of the Society of Jesus 'will always be
at the disposition of his Holiness' (*Constitutions*, 618). This is an
acknowledgement that the missions of individuals and groups within
the Church are part of the wider mission of the whole Church
which, as a community and through its leaders, sends them out for
apostolic service and supports them in it by prayer and celebrating
the Eucharist.

This brings us back once again to one of the central features of
Ignatius's approach to discipleship: the process of discernment of
spirits as a means of having the mind and heart of Christ in the
circumstances of everyday life. Hence when an individual or a group
in the Church has choices to make the Church community provides
the active context for discernment. Discernment about a path of
discipleship or about mission is not something which happens in
isolation from the wider community of the Church. On the contrary
the community participates. We have seen earlier in some detail
that personal discernment involves checking a possible course of
action with one's own past and present experience of God. But the
communal dimension is equally important, and the decision has to

be found to be in harmony with the history and experience of God of the faith community to which an individual person or group belongs. This is necessary and desirable in order to enable the Spirit of God to guide individuals and groups within and through the Church, and to prevent them from being isolated and led by 'false spirits'. The history of a community is the story of its experience of God through the ages and of its members' graced or sinful responses to God. The tradition of the community encapsulates and expresses in words or other symbols that experience of God. It also offers guidelines for action and criteria for discerning true from false action, so as to enable individuals and groups within the Church community to be led by the Spirit of God and to act as a check on false moves. This points once again to the fact that discernment is not a solipsistic activity. As well as subjective criteria for distinguishing true from false movements and attractions, namely the personal experiences of the individual, there are also essential external criteria contained in the tradition and practice of the Church. Discernment which neglects to take account of these lacks a vital dimension.

Discernment then means making choices within the context of a community of faith and in interaction with that community and its traditions. None the less in the process the individuals or groups who are faced with the choices retain their freedom. The community's traditions, which contain guidelines and criteria for right discernment, do not (or at least *should* not) of themselves dictate which choice or course of action a person or a group is to take up, to the exclusion of freedom of choice. Since from the nature of the discernment process the choices have to do with how an individual or a group is to follow the leading of God's Spirit in particular circumstances, and not simply with conformity or a mechanical application of precepts to a given situation, this freedom is essential, though some churches sometimes seem to find it hard to risk allowing it to their members.

If this freedom is granted, however, it entails accepting the possibility that individuals or groups within the community will sometimes act against the advice or traditions of the community or current trends within it or the authority of its leaders. On the

156

other hand for an individual or a group to ignore the community's guidance completely would be foolhardy and run the risk of isolation within the community or separation from it.[4]

This brings us to a consideration of the relationship between the individual and the community of the Church. The community supports and nourishes its individual members in countless ways, not least in the companionship of faith, prayer, love and in the members' shared sacramental life. On the other hand individuals and groups within the Church, in their turn, build up the community and the body of Christ by their lives of faith, their love, their participation in the community's life and their apostolic service both within and outside the community.

Sometimes of course tension arises in this relationship and breaks out into conflict. Historically this tension and conflict have been, and from time to time still are, an issue in Ignatian spirituality. In fact such a tension seems to be inevitably built into the nature of Ignatian spirituality itself, because it involves on the one hand a commitment to the Church and a high regard for its leaders and its magisterium, and on the other hand a commitment to personal discernment and decision-making. The combination of these two commitments in the real world, in a Church composed of fallible human persons, is a recipe for tension.

Ideally of course the two work together, because it is the same Spirit of God who guides the Church community, its leaders and its individual members in their paths of discipleship and apostolic service (Exx 365). But inevitably tensions exist, conflicts arise and individuals and groups even become marginalized within the larger community; through differences of perspective perhaps, or fear, blindness, an inability to listen to what is new, vested interests, lack of genuine openness to God, self-interest and other factors from which we are rarely wholly free and which easily become entrenched in individuals and groups. It is important to recognize however that the tensions and conflicts which arise in this way, with the results that they produce, can in fact be creative and open the way to progress and growth in the Church. That is not to deny that they are painful, often divisive, and that they can inflict permanent damage on the community and its members. But discipleship without tension and conflict is not possible, even if it were desirable.[5]

Ignatius was no stranger to such tensions, and his own conduct in them is instructive. There is no doubt about his commitment to the Church and the high regard in which he held its leaders and the Church's magisterium, in spite of the venal and scandalous personal lives of many prelates at the time. Nor is there any doubt about his commitment to personal discernment as regards both his own life and the Society of Jesus. His attitude to Church authorities was diplomatic and circumspect but also firm. He recognized their authority and the extent of his own commitment to obey (Exx 352–70). At the same time his obedience to Church authorities, like the provisions he made for obedience within the Society of Jesus, did not consist of an immediate and passive acceptance of whatever the authorities might decide. Dialogue in a context of mutual openness is an essential component of the exercise of obedience, though apparently not always possible or easy to sustain. Obedience which does not acknowledge the right of the one who obeys to represent his or her own position is totalitarian and unacceptable in the Church. When the decisions of Church authorities in important matters clashed with Ignatius's own convictions and especially with the outcome of his personal discernment, he obeyed, but not without protest. He used all possible forms of representation to make his own position known, respectfully but firmly, and the grounds on which he stood. And he used whatever legitimate means he had to influence the authorities and to have the decision changed, when he truly felt that was desirable.[6] Being committed both to the Church and to following the personal leading of the Spirit has led Ignatius and other individuals or groups into conflict. But it also offers a possible way of using tension and conflict creatively for growth.

The Eucharist

A fully Ignatian approach to the Christian life includes participation in the worship of the Church to which one belongs. Naturally there are great differences in understanding and practice of liturgy and sacraments between Ignatius's day and our own. He could not foresee, for instance, that his own approach to following Jesus would become popular in churches whose sacramental theology and practice are considerably different from those of the Roman Catholic Church. But there is also another notable difference between his age and ours. No doubt in the sixteenth century there was a communitarian dimension to attendance at Mass and the popular Eucharistic devotions. Nevertheless in his own writing Ignatius makes little reference to this but tends to focus on individualistic aspects of the sacrament. Along with many people at that time and since, Ignatius saw the Mass as a privileged occasion for personal devotion to God and to Jesus and part of the nourishment that each one needs in order to be able to live as a disciple of Jesus and to engage in service for the sake of the kingdom. By contrast in many churches today, including the Roman Catholic, this individual dimension is often present but is included in a fuller emphasis on the Eucharist as a community celebration. The Mass played a vital part in Ignatius's own personal life. During his stay at Manresa regular attendance at Mass and the Office in the monastery of Montserrat provided the liturgical setting which supported and nourished his personal prayer (Autobiography, 20), and gave him a taste for the Church's music. One of the extraordinary insights that he experienced while at Manresa had to do with understanding the presence of Christ in the Eucharist (Autobiography, 29). After he was ordained priest he waited several months before celebrating his first Mass so as to prepare himself more fully for the occasion (Autobiography, 96). And one of the notable features of his *Spiritual Diary* is the fact that at the time when he was writing the *Constitutions* of the Society of Jesus, celebrating Mass gave rise to profound insights and powerful movements of 'consolation' accompanied with many tears. Typical entries in the early part of his diary read:

During mass, there were several feelings in confirmation of what has been said: when I held the Blessed Sacrament in my hands I was impelled to speak and felt intensely moved from within;

that I would never leave him, not for all heaven or earth or . . .
then new impulses, devotion and spiritual joy. (s. 22, p. 36)

And: 'Throughout mass, very great devotion and many tears so
that quite often I lost the power of speech; all the devotion and
feelings had Jesus as their object' (s. 23, p. 37). So in his discernment of spirits with regard to important decisions that he had to
take at that time he noted especially what he experienced before,
during and after Mass each day. This he took to be confirmation
or otherwise of the choice he was making. The 'devotion' that he
felt at Mass therefore not only encouraged and nourished him
personally in his apostolic service but also actually helped to give
shape to the decisions he made, through his practice of noting and
interpreting the movements that he experienced.

Given all this therefore, it was natural that Ignatius should also
want his fellow Jesuits to find in the Mass 'devotion' and nourishment for their lives and work. He seemed to take it for granted that
Jesuits who were also priests would celebrate Mass daily, when that
was possible, and that became his own practice. In the *Constitutions*
he recommended that, as a general rule, Jesuits who were not priests
should attend Mass daily and receive Communion about every eight
days as part of their daily pattern of prayer (*Constitutions*, 261, 342).[7]
Like many other practices these too are to be subject to discretion
in consultation with the superior (*Constitutions*, 343). Ignatius also
recommended clearly that simplicity should be the hallmark of
Jesuit liturgies, and that members of the Society should not go in
for long elaborate ceremonies. This is in harmony with his determi-
nation that Jesuits' main work is apostolic service and that they
should be free and available for that. A commitment to elaborate
liturgies would hamper that freedom:

our members will not regularly hold choir . . . or sing Masses
and offices. For one who experiences devotion in listening to those
chanted services will suffer no lack of places where he can find
his satisfaction; and it is expedient that our members should
apply their efforts to the pursuits that are more proper to our
vocation, for glory to God our Lord. (*Constitutions*, 586)

Ignatius stipulates this in spite of the fact that he enjoyed the choral Office and Church music.

Contemporary approaches to the Eucharist

In many important respects our approach to and understanding of the sacraments, and the Eucharist in particular, are rightly different from those of Ignatius. This is in harmony with changes in our understanding of the Church and the Eucharist. Ignatius was no theological innovator; his understanding of the nature of the Church derived from first-hand experience of it throughout Europe and from accepted, orthodox theology of the time. It was perfectly natural for him therefore to take up the current image of the Church as an institution in which the hierarchy has the duty of providing nourishment for 'the faithful' by way of sound doctrine, good government and the administration of the sacraments as the principal 'channels of grace' and means of sanctification. Even the term 'administration' with regard to the sacraments suggests an institutional rather than a community image of the Church. And this image persisted as the main accepted model to the time of Vatican II.

Just as today we tend to emphasize that the Church is a community of Christian faith, hope and love, so also we lay stress on the sacraments as community events with participation by the members rather than as forms of nourishment 'administered' by the hierarchy. The Eucharist then becomes a communal celebration of our shared gift of life in Christ and of our common commitment to discipleship. This of course does not rule out the fact that the Eucharist is also a meeting with the Lord, nourishment and the means of our becoming holy. On the contrary, those aspects remain. The difference is that these various meanings of the Eucharist are appreciated in a communal context, as aspects of the life of a community which the community celebrates together, rather than as simply important events in the lives of individual Christians. And naturally the form in which we choose to celebrate the Eucharist expresses to a great or lesser extent the fact that it is an event in the life of a community in which the community participates as fully as possible. During the last thirty years or so Ignatian spirituality has taken up and incorporated this new way of looking at the Eucharist and the other sacraments. Ignatius's way of being a disciple of Jesus cannot be just a matter between the individual Christian and God, because Christian discipleship itself is essentially communal in that it means belonging to a community of faith. This communal dimension comes to expression 'in memory of him' in shared celebrations of our gift of life in Christ and of our common commitment to him and to his kingdom.

This communal dimension of the Eucharist finds valued expression nowadays even in the somewhat eremitical setting of the full Spiritual Exercises in seclusion away from daily life. Here, as we have seen, the person who makes the Exercises necessarily follows a very individual path. Most of the day is spent in silence and solitude except for the daily meeting with one's director, and even the common meals are taken in silence. In this setting the simple (usually daily) Eucharist together adds a very important communal element to the Exercises. It is an expression of shared gifts and commitment and of a common enterprise. Those who take part in it also experience it as a source of both giving and receiving support and encouragement for the time spent in solitude, and as a context for intercessory prayer for one another. Even if there is little overt personal interaction in the Eucharist in this context, it is still often experienced as a powerful symbol of shared gifts and shared purposes by which each individual is supported and nourished and contact with the wider Church is sustained.

The fact that Ignatian spirituality has been able and even eager to take up and incorporate these contemporary movements in theology and liturgy also points to another of its features which is worth mentioning. Ignatius's approach offers us the freedom to move along with, or even to instigate genuine movements in the Church when the Spirit blows, instead of being immobile and trapped by images, ideas and attitudes from the past that are no longer viable. Genuine developments in theology, liturgy, morality and all other aspects of the Christian life are by definition movements of the Spirit of God in individuals or groups. Ignatian spirituality, as we have seen, offers us the freedom and the means to distinguish between genuine and false developments in the Church and in ourselves and to follow what is discerned as genuine in these 'signs of the times'.

In this chapter I have sketched some images of the Church, ways of belonging to it and attitudes towards it that can be found in the Ignatian tradition both past and present. Implicit in this is my belief, based on current experience, that what Ignatius has to offer should not be thought of as relevant only to clerical or professed 'religious' groups in the Church, nor to men to the exclusion of women, but that it crosses these boundaries and has much to say to both women and men in any walk of life. This will be developed in the next chapter.

1 Ignatius's 'hierarchical' and 'institutional' concept of the Church is outlined in one of his letters, cf. *Letters*, pp. 367–72; and is noted by Jon Sobrino in *Christology at the crossroads*, p. 398.

2 The seminal book on the use of models in discussing the Church was Avery Dulles, *Models of the Church* (Gill and Macmillan, Dublin, 2nd edn, 1988). Dulles describes and compares several different images of the Church and points out the strengths and weaknesses of each. cf. also id., 'Imaging the Church for the 1980s' in his *A Church to believe in: discipleship and the dynamics of freedom* (Crossroad, NY, 1987).

3 Avery Dulles discusses the strengths and weaknesses of the 'servant' model in ch. 6 of *Models of the Church* (pp. 89–103).

4 cf. id., 'Institution and charism in the Church' in his *A Church to believe in*, pp. 19–40; and 'The meaning of freedom in the Church', ibid. pp. 66–79.

5 cf. Jon Sobrino, 'Unity and conflict in the Church' in *The true Church and the poor* (Orbis, Maryknoll, NY, 1984).

6 As superior general Ignatius was very tenacious in his opposition to a number of moves made by the Church authorities; as for example when it was proposed that some Jesuits should become bishops (cf. Dalmases, op. cit. pp. 193, 223, 229); or that Francis Borgia should be made a cardinal (cf. *Letters*, pp. 257–8); or that the Jesuits and the Theatines should merge into one congregation (cf. Dalmases, op. cit. pp. 285–7); or that Jesuits should have Divine Office in choir (Dalmases, pp. 170, 285–7).

7 The practice of daily communion of course was not common at the

time and did not become so until the time of Pope Pius X at the end
of the nineteenth century.

10

IGNATIAN SPIRITUALITY AND LAY CHRISTIANS

The development of a genuine spirituality which can be lived by lay Christians as distinct from clergy and religious has been dogged in the recent past and up to the present by a number of difficulties.[1] The first of these is a popular and widespread assumption about the Church according to which being a priest or religious is seen as an objectively 'higher' or 'better' form of the Christian life than that of the lay person. Religious and priests are seen as having a more elevated calling with a fuller and more single-minded commitment to holiness, discipleship and mission. The fact that when we talk about or pray for 'vocations' many of us still seem to mean exclusively priests and religious, as though they were the only or even the principal Christian vocations, is evidence that this view of the Christian life has by no means disappeared even now. As a result many excellent, committed lay Christians believe and feel, quite wrongly though understandably, that they are really second-class citizens of the Church and the kingdom of God, even though they form almost 99 per cent of the membership. The Second Vatican Council more than twenty years ago tried to rectify that mistaken view of the position of lay people in the Church by emphasizing the priesthood of all believers, the common call to holiness and to a share in the mission of the Church which belongs to all baptized Christians, but there is ample evidence that this perspective has not been universally accepted and assimilated.

Another popular assumption that has made the development of a living spirituality for lay people difficult concerns the importance of prayer for growth in holiness. It is commonly assumed that more prayer means more holiness; that in order to be holy a person has to spend long periods in prayer, and that the length of time one spends regularly in prayer is in some way a measure of one's holiness. This view possibly derives from the fact that historically most of the people who have been canonized by the Church did at some periods of their lives pray a lot, and that when they are held up as examples to the rest of us, it is often this aspect of their lives that is emphasized. The effect of this on many lay people is similar to the one I described before: even though they genuinely do not have time or opportunity for long periods of prayer, none the less they feel guilty, anxious and second class because of the common assumption that holiness and fully committed discipleship are not really possible without regular long periods of prayer.

The Ignatian tradition, as we have seen, questions this last assumption. Prayer, discipleship and holiness do of course go together. But the emphasis in Ignatian spirituality is discovering and responding to the presence and action of God in the circumstances of everyday life. Prayer obviously is necessary for this, but the amount and kind of prayer that each one undertakes is a matter for personal choice, with as much guidance as is needed or available, and the essential movement is towards an integration of prayer and the rest of life. One of the main considerations in our choices about times and styles of prayer is for each of us to determine the pattern of life that is realistically possible for us in the actual circumstances in which we live. God does not set us goals and programmes which we cannot actually achieve. God comes to us and we live out our Christian discipleship in and through the real circumstances of every day, and it is within those same circumstances that God makes us holy.

A third difficulty connected with developing a spirituality which actually arises out of the lives of lay Christians themselves is a not uncommon tendency to imply that the best patterns of prayer and asceticism for lay people are adaptations (or, some would say, watered-down versions) of monastic models. Obviously monastic models can provide a pattern of the Christian life that fosters growth in holiness and discipleship for lay people.[2] There is plenty of evidence to show that very many lay people have been helped enormously by monastic models. However, it is the imposition of a model or 'rule of life' from elsewhere that sometimes has harmful effects. By imposing an alien regime, we can force a lay person's life into a 'spiritual' mould that does not suit it, with a consequent binding and stunting of genuine growth. And once again, such an imposition can easily engender feelings of guilt and of failure before God when a person, in the absence of good guidance or other models, adopts a regime or 'rule of life' taken from the religious or monastic life, and then actually finds it impossible to live it out. The reason why it is impossible is not necessarily slackness or lack of discipline or commitment, though good people often accuse themselves of these things when they are not in fact at fault; it may be rather that the actual circumstances in which lay Christians have to live and work make such a plan impossible. Some may find monastic models fruitful, but lay Christians' discipleship and holiness are not intended to be less committed versions of clerical, religious or monastic life; they have to arise rather within the actual complex circumstances in which lay people live.

I believe that the Ignatian tradition addresses these difficulties. It is worth recalling at this point that Ignatius himself was a layman for the greater part of his life. He was not ordained priest until he was about forty-six years old and he did not begin the studies which would lead to ordination until he was in his late thirties. He was already about fifty when the Society of Jesus came into existence. And we should also remember that most of the crucial experiences which gave shape to his spirituality happened to him as a layman.

Ignatian spirituality does not depend upon the creation of a specialized setting such as a monastery or convent, nor necessarily upon a fixed pattern of prayer and ascetical practices (except of course in the specialized and very unusual setting of the Spiritual Exercises). It does, however, enable people to grow as disciples of Jesus and members of the kingdom of God. It is not a monastic or clerical spirituality. Though the last fifteen years of Ignatius's own life were dominated by the establishment of the Society of Jesus, most of whose members are priests, the Society of Jesus is only one historical form of Ignatian spirituality. One does not have to be a cleric or a religious, let alone a Jesuit, in order to live Ignatian spirituality. It is a particular way of approaching the Christian life which is open to people in any walk of life, lay or clerical, married or single, man or woman. That is not to claim that it appeals to everyone; clearly it does not, nor is it meant to.

But Ignatius's approach has such flexibility and breadth of appeal because, first of all, it goes beyond divisions of lay, cleric and religious to address the human person in his or her fundamental relationships with God, other people and the created world in which God has placed us. Secondly, it encourages and stimulates close personal and affective attachment to the person of Jesus. Thirdly, it provides the means for each person to learn to 'find God in all things', to respond to the leading of the Spirit of God in all the circumstances of his or her own unique life, however complex or even filled with pain and suffering they may be. These qualities together are the seeds of discipleship and growth in holiness.

Here is the basis of the current appeal of Ignatian spirituality to Christians in any way of life. It is sometimes said that the role of lay people, as distinct from clergy and religious, is to work within the 'secular' realm. But Ignatian spirituality, as I have described it, far from establishing or maintaining a division between 'sacred' and 'secular' times and places in life, actually points to the hidden but discoverable presence of God even in the most secularized and apparently godless situations. It also offers us all, whoever we are, the opportunity of allowing our own path of discipleship to emerge from within our own history and the circumstances of our own lives, and to make choices which give shape to the present and the future in line with that history and with what we experience as our own most authentic truth. In this way our deepest desires can be integrated: desires for ourselves and those near to us; aspirations and visions for the society and the world in which God has placed us, and the longing for God. So Ignatian spirituality offers us a chance to move towards a fuller integration of prayer and life, to change and to grow, under the influence of the gospel and the guiding, strengthening, creative Spirit of God at work in daily life.

Contemporary questions: mission

It would be a mistake to think that lay people meet no obstacles in their attempts to live out Ignatian spirituality at the present time. One feature which at least raises some questions is Ignatius's own constant emphasis on mission. We have already seen that apostolic service is greatly highlighted in the *Spiritual Exercises* from the end of the First Week onwards and especially throughout the Second Week. And we have noted that the second half of Ignatius's own life was dominated by mission: he dedicated himself to 'helping souls'; he became the founder and leader of a group of travelling evangelizers and later the builder and superior general of a religious order whose calling is apostolic service. Mission became his life, and it is for his direct and indirect contributions to apostolic mission in the Church that Ignatius is known and revered.

In our present-day experience this wholehearted emphasis on apostolic mission is a source of difficulty to many lay people who are otherwise greatly attracted to the Ignatian approach to Christian discipleship. It is not that they feel that the emphasis is wrong, clearly, but that it seems impossible for the majority of people. It raises questions like: how can I, a father or mother with a family to bring up and care for, dedicate myself wholeheartedly to apostolic service, to participating in the mission of the Church in a way that Ignatius and his companions did? And this kind of question evokes the fear that once again lay people are going to feel guilty, to see themselves and be seen by others as 'second class', because they cannot dedicate themselves to mission in the way that Ignatius seems to recommend.

If we are to try to resolve this difficulty, it is important to be clear about what we understand by mission. Once again we are in danger of using a two-tier model of mission according to which priests and religious are seen as the truly dedicated people who carry out the *real* mission in the Church, with lay people as a second-best, able only to share in this mission in the time they have free from the concerns of family and work.

The mistaken assumption underlying this view of mission is the belief that the Church's mission is solely or predominantly the concern of the hierarchy (with religious as co-opted members, as it were). I would want to say rather that the Church's mission is the mission of the whole people of God collectively and individually. It is witnessing to the good news of God incarnate in the saving life, death and resurrection of Jesus, 'this mystery that has now been revealed through the Spirit to his holy apostles and prophets' (Eph. 3:5). All baptized Christians are called to carry out this mission of witnessing to the good news in the circumstances in which God has placed them and in the way that they perceive themselves to be guided by the Spirit. For the majority of lay people this means a mission to witness to the good news and to the kingdom of God in the context of family life, work, friendship and the social, political and economic circumstances in which they find themselves. It cannot be emphasized too strongly that this in itself is mission; it is a vital share in the apostolic mission of the whole people of God, to which individuals, couples, families, groups and communities are invited to dedicate themselves wholeheartedly. It is obviously different in practice in many respects from the mission of religious and priests, but it is not a less demanding, less committed form of apostolic service; nor is it a 'secular' calling to which a more specifically 'sacred' mission has to be added. All the multicoloured forms of mission and service in the kingdom of God are essential and complementary in their diversity, and each in its own way gives glory to God.

Ignatius's own thinking does not seem to have been in radical disharmony with this view of mission. It is true that in accord with his own times and the long medieval tradition which fed him, Ignatius himself probably held that the religious life is objectively a better or higher form of the Christian life than that of the lay man or woman. This seems to be implied in the comparison he makes in the *Exercises* between 'the first state of life which is that of observing the commandments' and the 'second state, which is that of evangelical perfection' (Exx 135), by which he means the religious life. None the less, in the Exercises and elsewhere, what he is concerned about is not so much encouraging people to choose the 'higher' form of life, but rather offering guidelines by which each person can choose that way of life which expresses most fully her or his desire to follow Jesus. And if individuals have already chosen a state of life, he is ready to offer a process and direction by which they can decide how best to live to God's greater glory within that (Exx 15, 135, 150–7, 169–74, 189). What was important for Ignatius was not that people should choose what may be thought objectively better, but that we should be following Christ in the place where God wants us to be and open to respond to God generously there.

We have a good number of extant letters from Ignatius to lay people, especially women and men in positions of power and wealth. Sometimes he offered them advice about prayer and reading in these letters, but he also uses them as an occasion to encourage them in the right use of their wealth, status and power. His encouragement is based, once again, on what he saw as the 'principle and foundation' of the Christian life: the belief that the true purpose and fulfilment of each human life lies in using the gifts one has to give 'praise, reverence and service to God'. For Ignatius himself, that meant laying aside any wealth and status that he had in order to follow Jesus in poverty; but that is a very individual path, and most people are not called to walk along it. For the majority of those who have wealth and power the essential attitude, according to Ignatius's way of thinking, was to see these as gifts from God and to use them for the greater praise, reverence and service of God. This meant using them in the best interests of those people over whom the wealthy and powerful had some influence. So Ignatius might commend to them schemes for alleviating poverty, providing basic catechesis, fulfilling their role conscientiously as a local magistrate, founding a school, college or hospice, opening a women's refuge, taking an interest in a contemplative convent within their territory and so on. Occasionally, too, he recommends that individuals should set aside some time each day for prayer and religious reading, so as to sustain this essential openness towards using their gifts in the service of God and others.[3]

At the present time, too, Ignatian spirituality makes its own contribution to an understanding and living out of mission in the sense that I have sketched here. Personal affective attachment to Jesus helps us to assimilate his values, to express them in our attitudes and in how we live and work and deal with people, and to hand them on to our children and grandchildren. The desire for generous service of Christ and the kingdom, which Ignatius discovered in himself and looked for in others, impels people forward to discover and take up their own form of mission, whatever it may be. Familiarity with the gospels helps us to know and have the mind and heart of Christ in our day-to-day lives and in the important choices we have to make. The Ignatian focus on everyday discernment at the centre of the Christian life encourages people, whether lay, cleric or religious, to discover and effectively practise the form that their personal mission is to take. This obviously involves a full range of different lifestyles and activities in the Church 'for the sake of the kingdom', according to circumstances, needs and resources; from daily domestic tasks to sharing in great movements for liberation. It means taking care to use any power and influence that we possess, however humble and limited, for 'God's greater glory' and the good of others, perhaps especially those most in need, rather than in self-interest. And our sense of life as a gift 'from above' and our awareness of the presence of God at all levels of human existence and in all circumstances (Exx 235), even those which seem to carry the hallmark of sin, allow and encourage us to help others to discover that the kingdom of God is indeed very close to them, too, and to live for the 'praise, reverence and service of God'. All these are aspects of the mission of all baptized Christians to make the good news known by word and action.

Women and Ignatian spirituality

Another aspect of Ignatian spirituality which is raising challenges and questions among lay people, and especially women, at the present time is the fact that it originated with a man and grew largely within a group of men. And the most widespread form in which Ignatian spirituality has survived and spread is that of the Society of Jesus, a worldwide group of men living in single-sex communities. Is there not a danger that, unconsciously or deliberately, this is another form of male dominance, of patriarchy; that Ignatian spirituality tends to impose images of God and patterns of behaviour that are unhelpful to women and even unjust and oppressive? So far very little study has been done of this aspect of Ignatian spirituality, and I do not think that here I can do much more than raise the question and tentatively suggest one or two lines for further investigation.

In recent years the members of some of those congregations of religious women which were founded on an Ignatian approach to apostolic religious life have moved towards adopting more completely an Ignatian spirituality, embodied both in their day-to-day lives and in their ways of structuring their congregations. The fact that the different branches of Mary Ward's Institute of the Blessed Virgin Mary, and the congregations of the Faithful Companions of Jesus and the Irish Sisters of Charity have adopted and adapted the Ignatian *Constitutions* more fully in recent years suggests that Ignatian spirituality is in fact capable of appealing to women today as a congenial form of Christian discipleship.

In addition to that, we should recall that many women have played an outstanding part in the renaissance in Ignatian spirituality that has happened in the last twenty years, and some have been creative leaders and initiators. A vast number of women who are themselves sensitive to present-day issues about women in Church and society have made the full Spiritual Exercises fruitfully and found themselves 'at home' in them. Many of those, in their turn, have enthusiastically taken up the ministry of giving the Exercises, retreats and spiritual direction along the lines laid down by Ignatius, often with great success. And the popularity of Ignatian spirituality among women, both lay and religious, who are themselves often very aware of the questions which women are raising in the Church at present, implies that they do not on the whole see it as an instrument of patriarchy and oppression.

Moving on from that contemporary experience, we can also point to two features of the Ignatian approach to Christian discipleship which seem to me to be in tune with the questions being asked and the challenges being offered by women. The first has to do with the importance of experience. The criticism is justly made that in general in the Church women's experience as women has been ignored, even denigrated, and certainly not accorded the significance which is women's due. This is an aspect of a continuing injustice which affects the life of the Church at all levels: in the exercise of power, decision-making, the magisterium, the sacramental life and doing theology, to name but a few. Correlative to this is the fact that experience is becoming more and more widely recognized as a valid source for theology and spirituality. God is revealed in human experience, as well as in scripture and tradition, which are themselves the record of the Judaeo-christian community's *experience* of God. And women's experience is different from men's experience, of God and of life. Consequently, women ask questions of experience which are different from those which men ask, and in response find meanings and interpretations which are also different. Women's experience of life and of God, then, together with the theology and spirituality which develop by reflection on that experience, cannot be allowed to remain unacknowledged and ignored; it has to be given its rightful place, if all of us are not to remain impoverished.

One feature of the Ignatian approach to Christian discipleship that is clearly in harmony with these developments is the constant value placed on personal experience, whether of men or of women. Our personal and communal histories are the stories of God's dealings with us, and therefore a source for our knowledge of God, our theology. Ignatian spirituality repeatedly turns us back to our own personal and communal present experience as the place where we find God at work here and now, and as the basic ingredients for discernment of spirits and decision-making. The spiritual search for God is a search in contemporary experience, interpreted in the light of the gospel. Here we have to be sure that there is no unconscious or deliberate assumption that men's experience is privileged or superior. Each person's experience, in the context of our common, shared experience, becomes a place for discovering God, the day-by-day setting in which we can listen to the voice of the Spirit, and in which, as a result, conversion and growth can take place.

There is also a second feature in Ignatian spirituality that helps to put it in touch with the questions that women in particular

174

are raising today. That is the characteristic Ignatian focus on the interaction between the individual person and God, and the guidance offered for the development of this relationship: 'letting the creature deal with his or her Creator and Lord, and the Creator with the creature' (Exx 15). I have already commented at some length on this interaction in previous chapters and I will not repeat myself here. It is worth noting again, however, that both within the Ignatian Exercises and in the course of daily life, this relationship is seen as a means by which we grow in freedom. In particular, it is a context in which we discover and then learn to let go of the false gods, the false selves, the false attachments which block genuine growth and hinder us from moving forward in freedom.

In present-day experience, our relationship with God, in which we face God, ourselves and the world with some honesty, allows us to recognize, perhaps for the first time, that many of our false and distorted images of God and Church are associated with patriarchy, male dominance and the injustice meted out to women in Church and society. As a result, this relationship of 'familiarity with God' becomes the setting in which we can begin to discard those false images which act as obstacles to freedom. So the Ignatian emphasis on the importance of our relationship with God becomes one of the ways in which Ignatian spirituality responds to the challenges which women are making at the present time: it provides a context in which we can discover those images of God, self and Church, which are distorted through patriarchy, and the lack of freedom with which these images impede us. These discoveries once made and acknowledged, we can allow our patriarchal images to be changed, if we have the courage, and this can be another step towards greater justice and a fuller freedom.

To conclude I will simply repeat again that in itself Ignatian spirituality seems to have no major obstacle that prevents it from being a way of gospel discipleship for any baptized Christian whether lay, cleric or religious. That is not to offer it as a panacea, or to imply that Ignatian spirituality in fact appeals to everyone when it clearly does not. The features of Ignatian spirituality that I have mentioned in this chapter, however, would seem to recommend it to lay Christians, as well as to those religious men and women who are committed to an Ignatian approach by reason of the order or congregation to which they belong.

1 Strictly, male and female religious who have not received ordination are 'lay' people. But I am using the term 'lay' in a looser sense to refer to people who are not either clerics or members of religious orders or congregations. Strangely there does not seem to be a short, convenient term to denote this by far the largest and most important body of the Church's members.

2 In *Seeking God: the way of St Benedict* (Collins Fount, London, 1984) Esther de Waal shows how the monastic Rule of St Benedict offers a practical guide to holiness for lay people today.

3 See, for example, *Letters*, pp. 3–4, 31–2 (this letter is addressed to a bishop but the principle about use of wealth and position is the same), 39, 58, 91–3, 332, 415–16. The last of these letters is addressed to one of the secretaries of the Emperor Charles V. In it Ignatius expresses the hope that Philip II of Spain, who succeeded Charles V, may administer his new kingdoms 'to the greater glory of Him who bestowed them, to the good of all men, so as to merit for himself the crown of eternal glory' (p. 416).

FURTHER READING

For English translations of the Ignatian sources see p. 7.
For biographies of Ignatius in English, see p. 29.
This list does not include books and articles mentioned in the notes, with a few exceptions.

Abbreviation: *SSJ: Studies in the spirituality of Jesuits.*

BOOKS

Arrupe, Pedro, SJ, *A planet to heal* (Ignatian Centre of Spirituality, Rome, 1975).

Arrupe, Pedro, SJ, *Challenge to Religious Life today: selected letters and addresses,* I (Institute of Jesuit Sources, St Louis/Gujarat Sahitya Prakash, Anand, India, 1979).

Arrupe, Pedro, SJ, *Justice with faith today: selected letters and addresses,* II (Institute of Jesuit Sources, St Louis/Gujarat Sahitya Prakash, Anand, India, 1980).

Arrupe, Pedro, SJ, *Other apostolates today: selected letters and addresses,* III (Institute of Jesuit Sources, St Louis/Gujarat Sahitya Prakash, Anand, India, 1981).

Centrum Ignatianum Spiritualitatis (ed.), *The Spiritual Exercises of St Ignatius Loyola in present-day application* (Rome, 1982).

Clancy, Thomas H., SJ, *An introduction to Jesuit life: the Constitutions and history through 435 years* (Institute of Jesuit Sources, St Louis, 1976).

Clancy, Thomas H., SJ, *The conversational Word of God* (Institute of Jesuit Sources, St Louis, 1978).

Cusson, Gilles, SJ, *Biblical theology and the Spiritual Exercises* (Institute of Jesuit Sources, St Louis, 1988). Original French edition, 1968.

Documents of the Thirty-first and Thirty-second General Congregations of the Society of Jesus (Institute of Jesuit Sources, St Louis, 1977).

Documents of the Thirty-third General Congregation of the Society of Jesus, an English translation of the official Latin texts and of related Documents (Institute of Jesuit Sources, St Louis, 1984).

Egan, Harvey D., SJ, *The Spiritual Exercises and the Ignatian mystical horizon* (Institute of Jesuit Sources, St Louis, 1976).

English, John J., SJ, *Choosing life* (Paulist Press, New York/Toronto, 1978).

English, John J., SJ, *Spiritual freedom: from an experience of the Ignatian Exercises to the art of spiritual direction* (Guelph, Ontario, 1982).

Evennett, H. Outram, *The spirit of the Counter-Reformation* (Cambridge University Press, 1968).

Fleming, David L., SJ (ed.), *Notes on the Spiritual Exercises of St Ignatius of Loyola* (The Best of the Review, *Review for Religious*, St Louis, 1981).

Green, Thomas H., SJ, *Weeds among the wheat. Discernment: where prayer and action meet* (Notre Dame, Indiana, 1983).

Osuna, Javier, SJ, *Friends in the Lord* (The Way Series 3, London, 1974).

Peters, William A. M., SJ, *The Spiritual Exercises of St Ignatius: exposition and interpretation.* (New Jersey, 1967; Centrum Ignatianum Spiritualitatis, Rome, 1978).

Pousset, Edouard, SJ, *Life in faith and freedom* (Institute of Jesuit Sources, St Louis, 1980).

Rahner, Karl, SJ, *Spiritual Exercises* (London, 1965).

Schner, George P., SJ (ed.), *Ignatian spirituality in a secular* age (Wilfrid Laurier University Press, Ontario, 1984).

Stanley, David M., SJ, *The call to discipleship: the Spiritual Exercises with the Gospel of St Mark* (*The Way Supplement* 43/44, London, 1982).

Stanley, David M., SJ, *'I encountered God': the Spiritual Exercises with the Gospel of St John* (Institute of Jesuit Sources, St Louis, 1986).

Veltri, John, SJ, *Orientations*, vol. 2 (Loyola House, Guelph, Ontario, 1979).

Wulf, Friedrich, SJ (ed.), *Ignatius of Loyola: his personality and spiritual heritage 1556–1956* (Institute of Jesuit Sources, 1977).

SHORTER STUDIES, ESSAYS AND ARTICLES

Brackley, Dean, SJ, 'Downward mobility: social implications of St Ignatius's Two Standards', *SSJ*, vol. 20, no. 1 (January 1988).

Buckley, Michael J., SJ, 'Mission in companionship: of Jesuit community and communion', *SSJ*, vol. 11, no. 4 (September, 1979).

Byrne, Lavinia, IBVM, *Mary Ward: a pilgrim finds her way* (Carmelite Centre of Spirituality, Dublin, 1984).

Demoustier, Adrien, SJ, Calvez, Jean-Yves, SJ *et al.*, 'The disturbing subject: the option for the poor', *SSJ*, vol. 21, no. 2 (March 1989).

Edwards, Paul, SJ *et al.*, Essays in *From Loyola to La Mancha, The Way Supplement* 55 (Spring 1986).

Endean, Philip, SJ, 'Who do you say Ignatius is? Jesuit fundamentalism and beyond', *SSJ*, vol. 19, no. 5 (November 1987).

Futrell, John C., SJ, 'Ignatian discernment', *SSJ*, vol. 2, no. 2 (April 1970).

Ganss, George E., SJ, 'The authentic Spiritual Exercises of St Ignatius: some facts of history and terminology basic to their functional efficacy today', *SJJ*, vol. 1, no. 2 (November 1969).

Grogan, Brian, SJ *et al.*, Essays in *The Spiritual Exercises in daily life, The Way Supplement* 49 (Spring 1984).

Haight, Roger, SJ, 'Foundational issues in Jesuit spirituality', *SSJ*, vol. 19, no. 4. (September 1987).

Hewett, William, SJ *et al.*, Essays in *The retreat: imagination and guidance, The Way Supplement* 42 (Autumn 1981).

Hughes, Gerard W., SJ *et al.*, Essays in *The directed retreat, The Way Supplement* 38 (Summer 1980).

Ivens, Michael, SJ *et al.*, Essays in *Presenting the First Week, The Way Supplement* 48 (Autumn 1983).

Ivens, Michael, SJ *et al.*, Essays in *Some helps in giving the Exercises, The Way Supplement* 46, (Spring 1983).

Kinerk, E. Edward, SJ, 'When Jesuits pray: a perspective on the prayer of apostolic persons', *SSJ*, vol. 17, no. 5 (November 1985).

Lonsdale, David, SJ, 'Contemplative in everyday life', *The Way Supplement* 59, (Summer 1987), pp. 77–87.

McDermott, Brian, SJ, 'With him, in him: graces of the Spiritual Exercises', *SSJ*, vol. 18, no. 4 (September 1986).

McGovern, Arthur F., SJ, 'Jesuit education and Jesuit spirituality', *SSJ*, vol. 20, no. 4 (September 1988).

O'Leary, Brian, SJ, 'The discernment of spirits in the *Memoriale* of Blessed Peter Favre', *The Way Supplement* 35 (1979).

O'Leary, Brian, SJ *et al.*, Essays in *The Spiritual Exercises: Weeks Three and Four, The Way Supplement* 58 (Spring 1987).

O'Malley, John W., SJ, 'The Jesuits, St Ignatius and the Counter Reformation', *SSJ*, vol. 14, no. 1 (January 1982).

Rahner, Karl, SJ, 'Ignatius of Loyola speaks to a modern Jesuit' in K. Rahner SJ and P. Imhof SJ, *Ignatius of Loyola* (Collins, 1979).

Schineller, Peter, SJ, 'The newer approaches to Christology and their use in the Spiritual Exercises', *SSJ*, vol. 12, nos 4, 5 (September–November 1980).

Sheldrake, Philip, SJ, 'St Ignatius Loyola and spiritual direction I', *The Way*, vol. 24, no. 4 (October 1984), pp. 312–19; and 'St Ignatius Loyola and spiritual direction II', *The Way*, vol. 25, no. 1 (January 1985), pp. 62–70.

Veale, Joseph, SJ *et al.*, Essays in *Aspects of the Second Week*, *The Way Supplement* 52 (Spring 1985).

Veale, Joseph, SJ *et al.*, Essays in *The Ignatian Constitutions today*, *The Way Supplement* 61 (Spring 1988).

Yeomans, William, SJ *et al.*, Essays in *The place of discernment*, *The Way Supplement* 64 (Spring 1989).

INDEX